Women, Clubs and Associations in Britain

'A club is a weapon used by savages to keep the white woman at a distance.'
(George Augustus Sala, a founder member of the Savage Club)

Of the many and varied groups of people excluded from clubs and associations, the most commonly discriminated against is women. They have been excluded not only from West End clubs, including military clubs, but from working men's clubs and from sporting clubs. In retaliation, many women in Britain have set up their own clubs and associations, often though not always along the lines of male clubs, and have also striven to break down resistance to their joining 'men's' clubs on an equal footing.

Women, Clubs and Associations in Britain is a very readable survey of the historical background of women's clubs, drawing on a wide range of published and unpublished sources, and additionally, of associations like the Women's Institutes and Townswomen's Guilds. The authors also look at clubs and associations for girls, such as the Guides and the YWCA. It includes women organising for voluntary service outside the State and their complex relationships with men's clubs, and with bodies such as Rotary. And of course, there is the vexed and volatile matter of women's, men's and mixed sports clubs. This book is intended in the first instance for the general reader, but it will also be of use to students of social and women's history.

David Doughan MBE was Reference Librarian at The Fawcett Library (now The Women's Library) from 1977 to 2000 after a career in teaching and broadcasting; he continues to be closely involved with the Library. He has been a prominent member of the Women's History Network and a conspicuous contributor to women's studies and women's history, with special reference to suffrage history and periodical bibliography. Previous publications include *Lobbying for Liberation* (1980), *Feminist Periodicals 1855–1984* (1987) with Denise Sanchez, and the *Dictionary of British Women's Organisations* (2001) with Peter Gordon.

Peter Gordon is Emeritus Professor at the Institute of Education, University of London. He has had wide experience of teaching history and was a member of Her Majesty's Inspectorate of Schools for a number of years. He has written and researched on many aspects of nineteenth- and twentieth-century political, educational and social history and social policy, and is a Fellow of both the Society of Antiquaries and of the Royal Historical Society. Recent publications include the *Dictionary of British Women's Organisations* (2001) with David Doughan, and *Politics and Society: The Journals of Lady Knightley of Fawsley, 1885–1913* (2004).

Woburn Education series
Edited by Peter Gordon
University of London

Women, Clubs and Associations in Britain

David Doughan
and Peter Gordon

Routledge
Taylor & Francis Group

LONDON AND NEW YORK

First published 2006
by Routledge
2 Park Square, Milton Park, Abingdon, Oxon, OX14 4RN

Simultaneously published in the USA and Canada
by Routledge
270 Madison Ave, New York, NY 10016

Routledge is an imprint of the Taylor & Francis Group, an informa business

Transferred to Digital Printing 2009

© 2006 David Doughan and Peter Gordon

Typeset in Bembo by
HWA Text and Data Management Ltd, Tunbridge Wells

British Library Cataloguing in Publication Data
A catalogue record for this book is available from the British Library

Library of Congress Cataloging-in-Publication Data
A catalog record for this book has been requested

ISBN10: 0–415–36866–9 (hbk)
ISBN 10: 0–415–55135–8 (pbk)
ISBN10: 0–203–02901–1 (ebk)

ISBN13: 978–0–415–36866–7 (hbk)
ISBN13: 978–0–415–55135–9 (pbk)
ISBN13: 979–0–203–02901–5 (ebk)

Contents

Figures

Acknowledgements

The authors would like to acknowledge with grateful thanks the kind help and expert advice provided by friends, colleagues and others, with especial mention of the following:

Julia Cawthorne of the GFS Platform; the late and deeply lamented Virginia Clark for finding many recondite sources; Irene Cockroft, above all for checking the history of Soroptimist International; Margaret Courtney, Archivist of Girlguiding UK; Eileen Hawkins, Archivist of the YWCA; Ron Heisler for pointing us to eighteenth-century sources; Joan Huffman, especially for information on Lady Frances Balfour; Liane Langley of Goldsmith's College for information on the history of the Queen's Hall; Sarah Paterson of the Imperial War Museum Library; Colonel Christopher Steele; and Jennie Wethersbee of Inner Wheel. Thanks also to Charmian Seton Veitch, Emma Christie, and other members of the International Lyceum Club of London.

We also wish to express our appreciation to the staff of the following libraries for their helpfulness:

The British Library at St Pancras, the British Library Newspaper Library, the Imperial War Museum, the London Library, the University of London Library and The Women's Library.

We would also like to thank the secretaries of many clubs and officers of organisations for their unfailing kindness and patience in providing answers to our many questions.

Finally, our thanks to *Home and Country* and the National Federation of Women's Institutes, GFS Platform, YWCA England and Wales, Girlguiding UK and Solo Syndication, *Evening News*, for permission to reproduce the illustrations.

Abbreviations

ACWW	Association of Country Women of the World
AEWHA	All England Women's Hockey Association
AGM	Annual General Meeting
ATS	Auxiliary Territorial Service
BBC	British Broadcasting Corporation
CIU	Working Men's Club and Institute Union
CRAFA	Comrades of the Royal Air Force Association
CWS	Co-operative Wholesale Society
EFA	English Football Association
FANY	First Aid Nursing Yeomanry
FIFA	Fédération Internationale de Football Association (International Association Football Federation)
GFS	Girls' Friendly Society
GFWC	General Federation of Women's Clubs
HRT	Hormone Replacement Therapy
IOC	International Olympic Committee
IWCC	International Women's Cricket Council
MCC	Marylebone Cricket Club
MP	Member of Parliament
NCGC	National Council of Girls' Clubs
NFWI	National Federation of Women's Institutes
RAF	Royal Air Force
RIBI	Rotary International of Great Britain and Ireland
SI	Soroptimist International
TFL	The Fitness League
TG	Townswomen's Guilds
UEFA	Union of European Football Associations
VCO	Voluntary County Organiser
WAAC	Women's Army Auxiliary Corps
WAAF(A)	Women's Auxiliary Air Force (Association)
WCG	Women's Co-operative Guild
WI	Women's Institutes
WRAC	Women's Royal Army Corps

WRAF	Women's Royal Air Force
WRAFOCA	Women's Royal Air Force Old Comrades' Association
WRNS	Women's Royal Naval Service
YMCA	Young Men's Christian Association
YWCA	Young Women's Christian Association

LONDON LAUGHS ... *By LEE*

[No. 446.] UNIVERSITY WOMEN'S CLUB

" No, I'm afraid she's up at Oxford just now . . . but, of course, she may be sent down any day, n'know."

Cartoon by Lee, *Evening News*, 21 October 1935

Introduction

The theme of this book suggested itself to us as we were working on our *Dictionary of British Women's Organisations* (Woburn Press, 2001). One category of organisations that immediately stood out in terms of sheer numbers and variety was that of women's clubs, and we came to believe not only that they deserved more detailed treatment, but that the whole matter of women and clubs posed interesting questions that have seldom if ever been addressed except briefly, or in passing. As we proceeded, we found that our scope was becoming ever wider. For example, it is obvious that the Women's Institutes have much in common with the club type of activity; and if they are included, there is a strong case for including the Women's Co-operative Guild and the Townswomen's Guilds. Similarly, we felt that we should include the Soroptimists, which meant that we should look also at the Inner Wheel, which in turn involved at minimum some background on the Rotary movement, and the complex relations of Rotarian clubs and their 'womenfolk'. Thus we soon ran into problems of definition.

So what follows is not intended to be an exhaustive list of women's and girls' clubs, or indeed a completely comprehensive survey of clubs and their involvement with women; for example, readers will seek in vain for material on Toc H Women or the estimable Victoria League, and there are many other women's and girls' clubs of one kind or another that we do not mention. This is more a collection of case studies which we hope may serve as an illustration of the complex relations between women and clubs and associations of different types. Our initial proposal for this book was entitled *Sex War in Clubland*, but we rapidly discovered that this would be so gross a simplification as to distort the material we have discovered. It should be said that by no means all the sources we have used are original, although many are unattributed, being the result of personal experience over the years. We have also made extensive use of secondary works, so that this is less a series of new departures than a bringing-together of much work that others have done and published elsewhere along with original research that we have carried out ourselves. We are deeply indebted to a number of authors and organisations, who are acknowledged not only in the Bibliography, but in the source notes at the end of individual chapters, and in the case of a number of individuals who provided crucial aid at important stages, in our Acknowledgements. Of course this does not mean that if we have committed errors through indiscriminately 'lifting' material from others, or from misunderstanding or misquoting, that the fault lies with anybody but ourselves. In addition, the nature of these clubs, together with the nature of the sources and the location of the authors, means that there is a strong emphasis on London, only rarely alleviated by excursions into the provinces and even Scotland and Wales.

Although we trust that academics will find this work useful at least as a starting-point for their own research, it is meant more for non-specialist readers who we hope will find it illuminating, interesting and occasionally even amusing.

Sources

Our sources have been diverse in the extreme, including the daily, weekly, monthly and quarterly press from the eighteenth century onwards; parliamentary papers; clubs' and associations' own reports, and occasionally their internal documents; secondary works on clubs and associations; correspondence of individuals; and, as indicated above, personal information supplied by a number of individuals, who are thanked in the Acknowledgements. Details of all the published sources are given in the Bibliography. Since this book is intended for general readers as well as specialists, we have decided not to use footnotes or even endnotes, despite the arguments for both deployed in the *Times Literary Supplement* issues of May – June 2005. However, at the end of each chapter there is an indication of major sources used in its compilation. References to works in listed in the Bibliography are given in Harvard format, i.e., author or title and date.

Why clubs?

John Tibbs, in his *Club Life in London* (1866), opens with the statement, 'The Club in the general acceptation of the term, may be regarded as one of the earliest offshoots of man's habitual gregariousness and social inclination', and he traces the practice back to Athens and Lycurgan Sparta. Early in the eighteenth century, Joseph Addison, in *The Spectator*, put it more eloquently:

> Man is said to be a sociable animal; and as an instance of it we may observe, that we take all occasions and pretences of forming ourselves into those little nocturnal assemblies, which are commonly known by the name of Clubs. When a set of men find themselves agree in any particular, though never so trivial, they establish themselves into a kind of fraternity, and meet once or twice a week, upon the account of such a fantastic resemblance.

The first European to say explicitly that humans are social, or sociable, beings was probably Aristotle, in the fourth century BC, and even then he was almost certainly uttering a truism. However, what he meant by 'social' was 'living in towns', as part of a city-state. We are looking at a different kind of social interaction: one independent of state or church, participation in which is by free choice, not communal compulsion or dictatorial decree, but what is usually referred to as 'voluntary association'. Groups have thus historically been formed for a wide variety of reasons: to promote mutual interests (including political), to combine to pay for necessary expenses, to seek intellectual or moral improvement, or just to enjoy social gatherings, preferably of people who share similar interests, or who come from similar backgrounds. The most typical of these social groups are known as 'clubs' – though, as will be seen, other bodies not specifically called clubs have many features in common with them.

The term 'free choice' needs immediate qualification. Many such groups have systematically defined qualifications for membership so as to make sure that the right sort of people are included, and this is usually done by excluding, either intentionally or structurally, those who do not fit the criteria. To take a few random twenty-first-century examples: membership of the John Innes Society, with a number of club-like activities, is open to all who apply and pay their membership dues; the fact that meetings are always held in Merton Park, which tends to exclude anybody who lives a long way from London SW19, is incidental. Also, there are various other clubs and associations to which membership is dependent purely on a statement of common interest, an agreement to obey the rules, and payment of subscription. However, it is harder to become a member of many other associations. For example, to join a major West End club, applicants usually need to be proposed by one or two existing members, and even then may be blackballed for any or no reason. This ensures at least that new members will be acceptable to the existing membership, and also that they will probably be of similar socio-economic, political and cultural background: a recipe for homogeneity. And then, of course, some societies only select members by invitation: a discreet approach is made to a more-or-less unsuspecting person who, it has previously been decided, is The Sort of Person We Want; if they are willing, they are accepted, subject usually to undergoing a more-or-less complicated system of initiation, the most obvious and extreme example of this being the Freemasons. As Niall Murtagh recounts, many aspects of modern Japanese business culture, and of Japanese society in general, are an extreme instance of stressing like-mindedness above all else; apparently the Japanese language does not differentiate between 'different' and 'wrong'. Indeed, keeping out people who are different, not to say wrong, may be at least as important as getting the right people in. To give a facetious example, there is the old story of the two Welshmen who were stranded on the conventional desert island. When they were rescued, it was noticed that they had built three small huts. 'Well, they're chapels. The one on the right is mine and the one on the left is his.' 'What about the one in the middle?' 'That's the one we don't go to.' Or, as E.M. Forster put it rather more elegantly in *A Passage to India*, 'We must exclude someone from our gathering, or we shall be left with nothing'.

So who is excluded? Obviously, those who do not share similar interests; people to whom *The Ride of the Valkyries* is aural and mental torture are unlikely to want to join the Wagner Society. There are also those structurally selected on grounds of income: for example, a number of people who fulfil the criteria for membership of the Royal Overseas League might have difficulty affording the subscription. In a more intentional sense, members of the Carlton Club are unlikely to welcome somebody with a history of blackguarding Winston Churchill and Margaret Thatcher, while a working men's club may look askance at an application from a local sweatshop employer. And in the past at least such intentional exclusions have sometimes had a nasty aspect; for example, when in the USA in 1890 even the very high-minded and otherwise admirable General Federation of Women's Clubs decided to bar women of colour, in response to which a group of Black women set up the rival National Federation of Women's Clubs of America in 1896. Also Jews, Catholics and members of other ethnic or religious groups not deemed to fit into Anglo-Saxon clubbability are or have been excluded either explicitly or informally. Even when there are no general exclusions, individual aspirants may find themselves 'blackballed', an expression that derives from a traditional form of balloting members; when a nomination for membership was being voted on, members were issued with two balls: one black, to be put into the box for a rejection, and one white, for approval. Just one black ball in the box was all that was needed for a nomination to be rejected, even if all other members supported it. The term 'blackballing' is used for this sort of unanimous approval system, whether or not actual balls are used. 'Blackballing' is something that has happened to many prominent people who would on the face of it seem eminently qualified for membership of the club. To cite an instance from the early twentieth century: Lady Frances Balfour and other members of the highly intellectual, artistic and literary women's Lyceum Club proposed the famous actress Ellen Terry for membership, and were astonished to find she had been blackballed. Lady Frances discovered the identity of the blackballer and challenged her on this. The blackballer replied that she had nothing against Ellen Terry personally, but was simply worried about the sort of people she might attract.

Women and clubs

Categories of the excluded are many and various, but one category for exclusion has been more widespread than any other, namely, women. Why and how this has been the case is often less easy to establish than is assumed, and the way this exclusion has or has not been modified in recent decades is a complex issue. Traditionally, members both of élite men's clubs and of working men's clubs have regarded the club as a place to get away from female company, in keeping with the old separate spheres ideology according to which the man dealt with the public world, whereas women's domain was the home. In the case of sports clubs, women may be assumed to be too feeble to compete with men, hence liable to drive standards down. More seriously, as in the case of snooker and working men's clubs, they might start winning.

This is of course just one example of a general exclusion of women from public spaces. It is fairly well known that many pub landlords would refuse to serve women unescorted by a male until relatively recently on the grounds that they might be prostitutes touting for custom, not unreasonably, since if the police or those with influence wanted to deprive a landlord of his licence, this could be cited as a complaint. Much less well known is that in the 1960s similar thinking also formed the policy of the Wimpy Bar chain of fast food restaurants at least in the evening, as nurses coming off a late shift in uniform discovered to their amazement. On a larger issue it is sometimes forgotten how recently women were regarded by responsible bodies as at best second class citizens. As late as 1975 it was perfectly legal for building societies to deny professional women with respectable incomes a mortgage unless they could provide a male guarantor, and a few did just that.

So it should be taken for granted that quite late in the twentieth century discrimination against women was still at least in some quarters regarded as part of the natural order of things. Equally naturally, it should be acknowledged that at least some women fought back. As men's clubs developed especially in the eighteenth century, women attempted to find equivalent ways of socialising in other than covert informal ways: in other words, to gain access to public space. This was a campaign waged on various fronts. Attempts were occasionally made to breach the defences of men's clubs. More successfully, at least from the mid-nineteenth century on, while not letting up on the pressure on men's clubs, women began to establish their own clubs and associations outside the accepted system. There had already been attempts by women to use commercial and political initiatives to establish their presence – which is where we begin.

1 Early days

Debates and discussions

Clubs of one sort or another have been around at least in Europe since antiquity, though in ancient Athens and Rome they were usually highly informal; dining clubs and drinking clubs would in fact be more like a group of friends eating at each other's expense or organising rounds of drinks. This was a tradition that continued into the seventeenth century and beyond as successors of the clubs, sodalities, or societies of the Middle Ages. However, alongside these developments, there were more formal organisations. Some of these, also claiming ancient ancestry, are rather different from most clubs, the Freemasons being the most obvious example. Again, there have been bodies commonly referred to as 'clubs', but which have more in common with benefit clubs, or friendly societies – especially ancient Roman burial clubs, from which the Oddfellows among other bodies sometimes claim descent. In fact the Oddfellows can only be traced with any reliability back to the late eighteenth century. Female participation in these organisations may have been problematic; it certainly was for a long time among the Oddfellows, despite the fact that as early as the 1830s one of the objects of the Grand United Order of Oddfellows was stated to be:

> for insuring a sum of money to be paid on death of a member to the widow, or widower of a member, as the case may be or to the child or children, or to the executors, administrators or assigns of such member or members; or for defraying the expenses of the burial of a member or members, or of the husband, wife, child or kindred of a member or members.

Even so, as late as 1898, at the Annual Movable Committee of the Order of Oddfellows at Oxford, the Grand Master recollected 'the stern determination of our ancient brethren in the early days of the order to preserve it as an exclusively masculine institution ...', before noting that there were 72 female lodges, with a total membership of 3,551. On this occasion a resolution was passed to permit female 'branches', rather than just lodges, thus making women full members of the friendly society. However, this was somewhat qualified by another resolution to the effect that quarterly and travelling passwords should not be issued to female lodges, but that there should be a separate password circulated for use by female lodges only. The pretext for this was that many lodges were obliged to be held on licensed premises, and they did not wish to encourage young women to enter a public house. Despite it being pointed out that they appeared to be giving with one hand and taking away with the other, the resolution was passed by a large majority. A similar provision seems to have prevented women delegates from attending district meetings, but in 1901 this was abolished, on the ground that female lodges were now branches of the Unity. There will be many more examples later in this book of male ingenuity in finding pretexts for keeping females at bay.

Still, none of the above are what are usually understood by the term 'club', at least nowadays. So what are, or were, 'real' clubs, and where do they come from? According to our definition, which seems to be the most widely accepted, they are voluntary associations a major purpose of which is socialising; indeed, for many, this is their main or even sole purpose. Their development was not peculiar to Britain; late eighteenth-century Paris, for example, as well as such famous political clubs as the Jacobins, had among others a non-political social 'Club Militaire' for army officers. However, it was recognised even at this time that the British, or more specifically English, club was something different, for, as one Daniel Fordyce put it as early as the 1730s, 'we are of all nations the most forward to run into clubs, parties and societies'. Even then the English were regarded as a nation of joiners, at least in this sense, as individuals organising outside official authority; in Moscow the grandiose club on what was then as now called Tver Street was indeed the English Club. This has obviously continued to be the case, especially with women's clubs. In twentieth-century Europe France is of course an extreme case. There were post-revolutionary exceptions, such as the very upper-class élite Jockey Club, the English name of which gives the show away, but official France has never been particularly friendly to concepts of 'civil society', whether expressed by such Anglo-Saxons as Locke or indeed Michael Oakeshott, whose idea of a 'clubbable' society finds no resonance across the Channel; the French look very much askance even at Jürgen Habermas and his conceptions of what independent individuals gathering in unregulated groups can do. The idea of clubs as an example of Anglo-Saxon exotica is reinforced when women are concerned. When the French affiliate of the women's Lyceum Club was started in 1908, the very idea of a women's club in Paris was regarded by the French press as bizarre. In the 1920s, Suzanne Noel discovered similar incomprehension when she established a French Soroptimist group, as will be seen in Chapter 8.

The reasons why English club life developed somewhat separately, and flourished in a way different to that of European countries, lies at least in part in the Reformation. Before the 1530s, social and philanthropic life had been limited largely either to trade guilds, which had their own rather different development, or religious confraternities more or less under clerical control, as on the Continent. In England as a result of Henry VIII's reforms these confraternities withered, and under Edward VI they were legally abolished. This left a gap which was only slowly filled by new sorts of voluntary association, and it was not until the late seventeenth century that clubs as we know them began to emerge. Thus to a large extent English clubs are a fruit of the Enlightenment. They developed alongside learned societies and academies, and often overlapped with them. They were largely urban, and especially metropolitan; by the eighteenth century London clubs in particular were flourishing. This was a time when, for example, there were over 2,000 coffee houses in London, and they were the origins of the gentlemen's clubs we know today. Especially designated premises were sought after, such as White's (1730), Brooks's (1764) and Arthur's (1765) and were mainly devoted to talking, gaming, eating and drinking. However, they were, like their predecessors and continental contemporaries, exclusively male societies. Women were frequently lauded and toasted as club patronesses *in absentia*; as inspiring divinities they were not expected to set foot in profane masculine territory.

A rare exception to this situation occurred in Dublin in the Beefsteak Club in 1753. A club with this name had been established in London in the first decade of the eighteenth century, mainly for wits such as Sir Roger de Coverley and Sir Robert Steele. This was followed in 1735 by the Sublime Society of Steaks, founded by John Rich and the Earl of Peterborough in the Theatre Royal, Covent Garden, moving later to the Lyceum Theatre. The playwright and theatre manager, Thomas Brindley Sheridan, set up his own Beefsteak Club at his house in Dublin. Some 50 guests were invited and were either peers, MPs or other people of high social standing. Thirty of them accepted the invitation, dining at Sheridan's expense. He invited Peg Woffington, the celebrated Irish actress, who was then at the peak of her popularity, to join the company, and she was subsequently elected as their president. Sheridan and Woffington were the only actors who were members of the club. The proceedings were always light-hearted and at one meeting, when the Lord-Lieutenant of Ireland, the Duke of Dorset, was attending, Woffington recited a lengthy sycophantic poem dedicated to the Duke.

Shortly after this, and more significantly, in 1765, a club for both sexes was established in London at Almack's Rooms. Ladies were nominated and chose the gentlemen and vice versa; nobody could exclude a lady, no gentleman a gentleman. However, if a married woman was elected, her husband automatically became a member; the same privilege was not extended to the wives of male members. Dinner was served at meetings; this was followed by supper at eleven and then card playing began in earnest. Its more high-minded successor was the Female or Coterie Society, which in 1775 moved out of Almack's Rooms into Sir George Colebrook's more than adequate house in Arlington Street, for which the Society paid a cool 13,000 guineas (this may have been unwise). The premises were sumptuous, with separate dining, parlour and card rooms, as well as 'bed-chambers'. Although the actual management was controlled by men, namely Robert Sutton and later James Cullen, a good many high-status women, including titled ladies, served on the club's committee. Interestingly, in the subscription lists, when married couples were listed together, the wife's name was listed before her husband's. Also, women constituted nearly half of the more than 500 who attended club functions (fully paid-up members were another matter). Still, although women were an important part of the club, it was nevertheless male dominated. This had a great deal to do with the position under the law of women, particularly married women, who by the laws of coverture had no legal standing in their own right, and hence could not sign the necessary contracts involved in the effectual management of the club. In the case of the Coterie, this was rather fortunate for them, since when the club closed in 1777, they were not involved in the ruinous financial consequences, unlike Lord Melbourne, among others. Financial problems, together with unwise investment in luxurious premises, is a theme we shall meet later.

However, upper-class social clubs of this kind were by no means the only sort of club that had come into existence by the 1770s. Many clubs were specialised, either by profession (e.g. the Architects' Club) or by intellectual interest (e.g. the Musical Society at the Castle Tavern). Musical societies in fact spread widely, and attracted women especially, not always to the pleasure of male members, as when men of the Calcutta Harmonic Society left to form their own 'Catch Club', which the ladies derisively named the 'He-Harmonic'. There were also overtly political clubs, particularly of a radical persuasion: they participated in the American Revolution, and played a crucial role in the French Revolution, especially the notorious Jacobin Club. In Britain they were less earth-shaking, but still had an effect on society. The most common association of this type from the 1750s onwards was the debating society, or club. Such clubs usually seem to have been commercial ventures, and charged admittance; the payment often appears to have included drink, which was most frequently porter. Still, despite their appearance of mere entertainment, they were the main forum where men outside the upper classes could publicly air their views on politics, religion and society in general. Indeed, they were not despised by men like Edmund Burke and the younger Pitt who looked to make their mark in politics, since they gave them an opportunity to hone their public speaking skills. Initially these clubs strongly excluded women, since women were supposed to be incapable of serious thought and discussion – as Pope had put it in his *On the Characters of Women*:

> No Thought advances, but her Eddy Brain
> Whisks it about, and down it goes again.

And of course the contemporary Dr Johnson made his famous comment on the idea of a woman preaching: 'like a dog walking on its hinder legs. It is not done well; but you are surprised to find it done at all'. Also, depictions of supposed female societies in comic papers and on the stage were always derogatory, with the speakers reducing every topic to clothes and fashion, screaming at each other, tearing each other's hair, and so forth.

Another factor discouraging the attendance of women was the often uninhibited nature of the club meetings, when 'good order and decency' were not always observed (the provision of porter may have contributed to this). So it is scarcely surprising that there was strong resistance to allowing women to participate in what was meant to be a facility for serious discussion, however heated and boisterous. In the 1750s there were some attempts to include women in more respectable types of public speaking, first by an institution briefly called The Temple of Taste in 1752, which allowed women to attend public debates, though not to speak. Then in 1754 and 1755 the actor and coffee-house proprietor Charles Macklin gave a series of lectures called 'the British Inquisition', mainly on acting and playwriting, followed by debate, open to both sexes, and judging from contemporary satires, some women may actually have taken part. However, these brief attempts were exceptional, and the rule of female exclusion remained.

By the 1770s this was beginning to change. The reasons for this are complex, and appear to include an improvement in public manners and an increasing acceptance of women in public venues, such as coffee houses. Additionally, women were taking an active interest in education and 'elocution' – in other words, the techniques of public speaking. The Thomas Sheridan mentioned above was a noted speaker on elocution, and had sometimes in the 1760s given elocution courses specifically to women. This was a period of considerable political ferment in Britain, and even more so elsewhere, and women were as eager as men to express their opinions. At first, as in Birmingham in 1774 and at the Coachmakers' Hall Society in London three years later, women were merely admitted as observers, and sat either in a separate railed area or in a gallery; however, they did not pay to attend. As *The General Advertiser* put it in 1778 in its account of Coachmakers' Hall: 'A number of ladies attended in the gallery, who were exceedingly attentive, and made a beautiful appearance'. The presence of women was also assumed to encourage the polite sober conduct that would attract a respectable clientèle previously discouraged by the rowdiness of debating societies. Despite the assumed passive and even decorative function of women, societies that allowed women's attendance, albeit not participation, did in fact meet with considerable success, and by the end of the decade most new debating societies admitted women as 'auditors'.

Then came the extraordinary year of 1780. In the course of that year there was a sudden surge in campaigns for political reform and this, and the later campaigns against the Catholic Emancipation Bill, culminating in the Gordon Riots, had led to a considerable growth in the number of debating societies in general. In particular, there was a marked increase in the number of women attending debates – so much so that in 1780 the debating society proprietors started to charge them the same price as men for admittance, no longer relying purely on their supposed decorative and civilising function. Some new societies went further. The Academy of Sciences and Belles Lettres, at Carlisle House, Soho, included a library, the equivalent of seminar rooms for group discussion and tuition, and tea and coffee rooms, as well as the main debating hall. It was considerably more expensive than most debating societies – entrance was 2s 6d as compared with the 6d charged by Coachmakers' Hall – but nevertheless it attracted significant numbers, of women as well as men; debates in February and March 1780 drew audiences of well over 1,000. In March another society opened at the Casino Rooms, Great Marlborough Street, and the 'Palladium' at Freemasons Hall soon followed, both admitting ladies. These three new societies were actually advertised not merely as debating clubs but as educational institutions, or at least ones providing 'rational amusements'. Elocution and oratory were high on the agenda. Some other societies followed suit, and increasingly the segregation of women was abandoned mainly because of practicalities; the number of women paying to attend had become too large to keep in a gallery. Nonetheless, not all women were happy with mixed seating, referring obliquely to the consequent opportunities for sexual harassment by predatory males.

The financial factor seems to have acted as a spur to demands for active participation. If women were to pay the same rates as men, many came to feel that they should no longer be prevented from participating. And indeed in February 1780 the first women's debating society, La Belle Assemblée, opened. Its initial meeting in the Haymarket, London, was chaired by a clergyman, men and women had segregated seating, the fee was 2s, and the motion, debated by ladies only, was 'Whether oratory is, or should be, confined to any sex'. As it happened, the segregation of the audience was rapidly modified to allow a certain amount of 'promiscuous' (i.e. unsegregated) seating. Another interesting feature was that speakers were permitted to wear masks or dominos. The location of La Belle Assemblée is interesting; in her *Gender and History* article Mary Thale points out that among other things it was in theatreland, and the performances in the debating chamber had something of the theatrical about them, although this could be said equally of other such societies, especially Coachmakers' Hall. It seems to have attracted at least some women of fashion, but there appears to be no indication of its class composition, or indeed actual names of the women involved, who in contemporary reports are referred to by initials if at all. Other debating societies for ladies sprang up immediately, notably the Female Parliament (at the Casino) and two societies called 'The Female Congress', one in Kensington, and one later in the year in Cornhill in the City of London; Carlisle House also provided a series of debates specifically for ladies.

Motions discussed at women's societies, or those where women's presence was encouraged, tended to differ from the more obviously political motions debated at purely male societies. Marriage and courtship loomed large. At La Belle Assemblée the question was put as to whether fine natural sense or extensive learning was 'the most amiable accomplishment in Women' (the vote went to natural sense), and 'whether is the inclination greater in spinsters to be married or married men to be single?', and a suggestion made that bachelors should be taxed. At Coachmakers' Hall the issue was whether mental or physical charms were more likely to induce men to marry. However, these were by no means the only topics discussed; for example, women's education came up frequently. Another topic raised more than once was the issue of male encroachments on such female occupations as millinery, obviously much resented, which may give some indication that the audiences were composed at least in part of women of the artisan class although man-midwifery may also have been resented. On one occasion, the audience who had voted in favour of restricting men's encroachments proceeded to draw up a petition, to be signed by women only, to be presented to Parliament. Going further, at La Belle Assemblée the issue of women's voting rights was raised, and even whether women should be eligible to sit in Parliament, perhaps the earliest time this issue was explicitly raised in Britain. On another occasion a motion regretted 'the precluding of the Fair from the privileges of Civil Society'. Mary Thale suggests that the number of feminist topics discussed might have been greater if the choice had depended on the speakers, rather than the paying audience. It tends to be assumed that discussion of women's rights did not seriously begin before Mary Wollstonecraft, although this is far from the case; the appearance of eighteenth century publications on this subject by such writers as Mary Astell and the anonymous 'Sophia', who in 1739 began a controversy in print on this topic, is simply among the more visible indications of a growing unrest. In any case, women speakers did not by any means restrict themselves to 'women's issues'; on at least one occasion, the Government and King George III came under attack from women. The women who raised and discussed these questions obviously had some education, as it was reported by some men, apparently with a degree of surprise, that the level of speaking was high.

Still, by no means everybody was happy to hear women speaking. One anonymous correspondent, 'Indignus', writing to the *Morning Post* and the *Morning Chronicle*, was particularly vocal, and repeated a claim often made: 'that these female Orators were any Thing more than the *hired* reciters of a studied lesson'. Even if this were not so, he reckoned, 'It would be very little to their honour', for 'Would not such Assurance and Effrontery render them absolutely disgustful?' Be that as it may, in 1780 at least, a considerable number of paying listeners were happy to indulge their disgust, and take the women at their face value as unhired spontaneous advocates of their causes, much as the men were.

All the same, by the end of 1781, all of the women's societies had disappeared. La Belle Assemblée closed in March of that year, and the last club inviting women to debate closed in the November. Indeed, many men's societies go into a similar decline at this time. The reasons for this appear to be complex, and have much to do with the decline of the movement for political reform. Historians tend to dwell on the influence of the Gordon Riots, quoting especially Edward Gibbon's *Autobiography*: 'the flames of London, which were kindled by a mischievous madman, admonished all thinking men of the danger of an appeal to the people'. By 'all thinking men' Gibbon obviously meant the wealthier classes, the sort who could happily pay the shillings, rather than pence, demanded by the societies where women played a part. But the fact, already noted, that these societies or clubs were above all commercial ventures definitely had an influence in their rapid decline. The wealthier patrons did not want to be associated with anything that smacked of radicalism. So it came to appear that women's involvement was simply the result of a freakish whim of fashion, and when society settled down to its normal state, female speaking and female clubs or societies would be looked on as a passing aberration.

Only that was not what happened. The immediate heirs of these female debating societies turned out not to be women's social clubs, which in Britain at least appear to have gone into abeyance for another couple of generations, although in the French Revolution political clubs like the Cordeliers, the Minimes and especially the Société Fraternelle des Patriotes des Deux Sexes, admitted women; this distinguished them from the Jacobins, who relegated women to home and childbed. In Britain the legacy of late eighteenth-century women's organisations, and the valorisation of women speaking in public is partly to be found in the revolutionary tradition of Mary Wollstonecraft, and in the early nineteenth century it was represented by a variety of radical women like Eliza Sharples Carlile, wife of the radical Richard Carlile, who was known as 'the Lady of the Rotunda', from the venue where she regularly spoke, and who in 1832 edited the political women's paper the *Isis*; and Anna Wheeler, who with William Thompson composed the *Appeal on Behalf of One Half of the Human Race* (1825). Later this tradition was continued by the women Chartists. However, there were other successors, represented by the more respectable reformist activities of Hannah More and Sarah Trimmer, and the female campaigners for the abolition of slavery, despite the fact that the leading abolitionist William Wilberforce disapproved of women campaigning in public. Another factor that may influence outcomes is that almost all of the above has focused on London. In the provinces the situation was not necessarily as clear-cut. Traditions of women debating continued at least in Birmingham and Edinburgh as late as the 1870s, and women's political activity in the Manchester area famously long after that. And, as we shall see, although the first recorded social club in Britain specifically for women appears to have been founded in London in 1860, Worcester and other provincial centres were not far behind. But that is in Chapter 4.

Major sources for this chapter

Peter Clark's landmark study *British Clubs and Societies 1580–1800* has been extremely useful, as have two remarkably detailed and informative articles on the situation in 1780 by Donna Andrews and Mary Thale, in *The Historical Journal* and *Gender and History* respectively. J.F. Molloy's *The Life and Adventures of Peg Woffington*, J. Dunbar's *Peg Woffington and the World* and M. Griffiths' *Clubs and Clubmen*, in addition to periodicals cited in the text, have also provided many helpful leads.

Clark's work in particular deserves reading in its own right as a major study of an important aspect of early modern British society that not only touches all the right academic bases, but is accessible to the non-specialist reader.

2 Men and their clubs

Gentlemen's clubs

Clubs are assumed to be an essential part of civil society, and thus essentially British; for example, by virtue of their independence of political control and their particularity they are supposed to be in complete opposition to what Pierre Rosanvallon, among others, calls the 'Jacobin' model of centralised national state-controlled association prevalent in France. This is of course at best a half-truth, but it has profoundly influenced popular conceptions. As late as the early 1960s it was widely assumed outside Britain that every Englishman belonged to a club, and this was brought home vividly to one of the authors in France, when he was asked what his club was; it was clear that a reply such as 'Kirkhamgate Working Men's Club' would only result in confusion and bewilderment. This was obviously due to the fact that much French knowledge of the English at the time was still derived from English upper-class literature of the early twentieth century, as well as from Pierre Daninos' Major Thompson, the fictional military man resident in France who explains the English upper classes to the French. Indeed, for many British people, the concept of a 'men's club' still automatically conjures up old soldiers in leather armchairs not passing the port to starboard, and 'Clubland' means a specific area of London's West End. For gentlemen's clubs are generally, and fairly accurately, assumed to have been mainly London-based; even though many provincial centres had (gentle)men's clubs, they usually stipulated that members of recognised London clubs could automatically become at least temporary subscribers, as can be gathered from early twentieth-century Ward Lock guides, among other sources. For men of a certain class, membership of one or more London clubs was effectively a social necessity, to be put on one's visiting card, whether or not much use was made of the facilities, although many clubs did provide a cheaper alternative to an hotel for those based outside London; and it could be useful as an accommodation address. But essential it was. For example, at least as late as the Second World War, it was expected that regular army and navy officers would automatically join a London club, if only 'The Rag' (the Army and Navy Club, of which more in Chapter 3). Flying officers would join the RAF Club ... but that was another matter. There were class gradations within these clubs as well. So these 'gentlemen's' clubs are the clubs that we shall deal with first, before coming to the equally interesting situation of working men's clubs.

Figure 2.1 The Great Subscription Room at Brooks's, St James' Street, London, 1808

It has been well stated that the club is based on two ancient British ideas – the segregation of the classes, and the segregation of the sexes. The range of clubs catering for different interests was and is enormous. White's, in St James's, the most aristocratic of them all, is the most exclusive. Brooks's, nearby, established by Charles James Fox, was the home of Whig aristocrats. It was notorious as a gambling place, as Horace Walpole wrote, 'where a thousand meadows and cornfields are staked at every throw, and as many villages lost as in the earthquakes that overwhelmed Herculaneum and Pompeii'. Another club with political origins was the Reform, set up by those who supported the 1832 Reform Act, whilst the Carlton has a totally Conservative membership. Perhaps the best known club is the stately Athenaeum in Pall Mall, which has been described as 'home for all the arts and sciences except gastronomy'. It was *de rigueur* at this club that members were not disturbed. It was rumoured when Michael Faraday died in his chair at the Athenaeum, he had lain there unnoticed under a newspaper for three days.

There were and are also what might loosely be called the cultural clubs, such as the Garrick, originally named after the actor and a haunt of the legal fraternity; the Savile, memorably called by Oscar Wilde 'a real republic of letters, not a sovereign among 'em'; and the Travellers', whose members include both diplomats and explorers. An original condition for candidates for the club was that they must have travelled out of the British Isles to a distance of at lest 500 miles in a straight line. As late as 1965 it could be said, ' The chief tradition of the Travellers' is that members do not speak to each other'. Writing in 1911, Ralph Nevill described a typical club member: 'Such an individual was perfectly content with his existence. Quiet, comfort, good living, freedom from responsibility and anxiety, were the great objects of his life, "and, begad, you don't get that by marriage"'. The proximity of clubs to one another which make up Clubland – mainly Pall Mall, St James's Street and Piccadilly – makes multiple membership easy. Though useful for networking purposes, the expense can be a deterrent; few could match Lord Louis Mountbatten, who could boast of belonging to 16 clubs.

Many men of the upper and wealthier classes in Britain were, in the late nineteenth and early twentieth centuries, known as clubmen. The extreme example of clubmen's obsession was parodied by Thomas Hood in a supposed female complaint about the disastrous effects of clubs on family life:

> One selfish course the wretches keep;
> They come at morning chimes
> To snatch a few short hours of sleep –
> Rise – breakfast – read The Times –
> Then take their hats, and post away,
> Like Clerks or City scrubs,
> And no one sees them all the day –
> They live, eat, drink at Clubs!

And, of course, women could not follow them there.

Exclusion from membership, as will be seen later, was not merely confined to women; for instance, the United Oxford and Cambridge University Club did not admit as members those who were graduates of London University. A more graphic example was the rejection in 1910 from membership of The Club, an exclusive Oxford dining group, of two leading politicians, Winston Churchill and F.E. Smith. As a result of this snub, in the following year the two men set up a rival group called The Other Club, consisting of 50 members, of whom not more than 24 were to be MPs.

Women and London clubs

According to George Augustus Sala, a founder member of the Savage Club, 'A club is a weapon used by savages to keep the white woman at a distance'. Other less extreme examples of this attitude, which was obviously widespread, have already been given. Indeed, the reasons given by clubs and their members for their reluctance to admit women to full membership have varied little in substance over time, though recently, more complex, sophisticated and often contradictory arguments are put forward. From the 1880s, when women's clubs began to burgeon, clubmen tended to regard females who joined them as untypical of their kind. John Galsworthy, in his novel *The Man of Property*, describes Mrs MacAnder, a friend of the Forsytes, as follows:

Dressing tightly and well, she belonged to a Woman's Club, but was by no means the neurotic and dismal type of member who was always thinking of her rights … It was generally felt that to such women as Mrs. MacAnder should we look for the perpetuation and increase of our best type of woman. She had never had any children.

The perceived differences between men and women's clubs were reinforced by a member of the Garrick and golf correspondent of *The Times* for 39 years, Bernard Darwin, who wrote about women's clubs:

> Clearly, such clubs have supplied a much felt want, but at the same time it may be suggested that women are not, or perhaps it is merely that they have not yet had time to become, quite as clubbable as men. It may be merely that they are less fond of good things to eat and drink, and less given to sitting on their shoulder blades in deep armchairs. It is almost certain that they are as a whole more economical in the matter of solid, lazy comfort.

A more frank comment on the matter was reported by one Carlton Club member when recently faced with the threat of the admission of women: 'I have nothing against women having their own clubs, but this idea that everyone can go everywhere and there is nowhere men can go on their own is very annoying'. Similarly, a member of the Royal Aero Club once told its Secretary, 'I don't want to belong to a club where my wife is a member'. It was even rumoured that one club which had capitulated to the notion of mixed membership displayed a notice: 'Members are requested not to bring their mistresses into the Club unless they happen to be the wives of other members'. Two other arguments have been put forward for preserving men only clubs. The first is that a mixed club might be handicapped where a merger with another club is contemplated. The second was advanced in 1986 by the historian of the Garrick on the question of full membership for women:

> There seems, for better or worse, little chance of a vote in favour at present. But as night follows day, even in Garrick Street, the subject will be aired from time to time in the future. Or perhaps, if offered full and equal membership, women will not want it.

There is something in this last point. To quote John Gibb on golf clubs in a 2002 edition of *The Spectator*:

> Accepting women as full members into private clubs has been a tricky issue. The response to the question, 'Why can't women vote at the annual general meeting or use the men's bar?' is, 'Because they don't want to'. There is some justice in this. Women's memberships are generally significantly cheaper, and the feeling among the girls is, 'Why shouldn't the old farts have their own corner of the club? At least it keeps them out of the way'.

Also, some of the traditional West End men's clubs have been noted for the bizarre behaviour tolerated in some of their members, which it is assumed would be unwelcome to ladies. Juvenile horseplay seems to have been fairly common, but sometimes this sort of misconduct went further. For examples of the more extreme sort of misbehaviour, in *A House of the First Class*, Binns *et al.*, the historians of the Travellers' Club, relate how a member in 1858 deliberately set fire to the wainscot in the coffee room, and in 1905 another member shot himself in the Billiard Room, not only blowing out his brains but tearing the green baize of the billiard table, which prompted the reported comment of the then chairman, 'A gentleman commits suicide in the lavatory. We shall make sure he *never* becomes a member of another club'. However, it is not only women who might be deterred by such behaviour and the attitudes implicit in it; and in the case of differential subscriptions many women would still like to have the choice of whether or not to take the more expensive membership, and have full privileges, and would shrug off the disadvantage of the company of boring old men, or even suicidal lunatics.

If the arguments for marginalising women as members carried weight, it is equally interesting to see how this worked in practice. The term 'ladies' was and is used rather than 'women', a term not always appreciated by those involved. An instance of this occurred some years ago at the Law Society, which then had a rule that women solicitors could take their fathers into the Dining Room as guests, but no other female member of the family. One solicitor's father, on being told by a waiter that he could not entertain a lady guest for lunch, retorted, 'My daughter is not a lady. She is an articled clerk'. Ralph Nevill also recalled that up to the late nineteenth century, 'it was not at all the thing to raise one's hat to a lady whom one knew, should she pass the Club window'. Additionally, as Peter Clark points out in his book on early clubs and associations, 'Conventional stereotyping of women as vain and silly meant that they were widely seen as unable to take part in that informal intellectual conversation which was regarded as the essence of club activity'.

Clubs varied from one to another in ways of excluding women from participation. At the Athenaeum in the nineteenth century, they were confined to a separate building, once owned by Gladstone's father, and were only allowed in the main building for soirees on Wednesday evenings. Until 2002, women guests, including members' wives, took lunch in the Underground Room whilst men ate in the expansive ground floor restaurant. At the Reform, until 1973 women were admitted to take dinner on Saturday nights only. At the Savile, women guests were not allowed to enter the smoking room when gentlemen were reading. In the 1990s, women from reciprocal clubs were admitted into the building but barred from the smoking room and the cocktail bar. There was no telephone available for women guests at Pratt's in the 1960s. Plans to build a Ladies' Wing was mooted in the 1950s at Brooks', but this scheme was soon abandoned. Up till recently, the United Oxford and Cambridge Club admitted women as guests but they were not permitted to use the Members' Bar, the

Library and the Grand Staircase; similarly, up till 1983 lady visitors to the
Liverpool Athenaeum were required to use the lift, not the stairs. The Great
Staircase is also out of bounds for women at the Carlton, except for Royalty.
Whilst the same rule exists for the Library at Brooks's, this rule was only once
broken. In 1938, Queen Mary paid a secret visit to the club, and when escorted
to the Library by her equerry, it is recorded, 'To her consternation, the then
Duke of Devonshire, at full length on a sofa, opened a bleary eye and exclaimed,
"My God, a woman!", then jumped to his feet with "Ma'am!"' Clubs of a more
reformist bent have usually been more open to women, at least as guests or
visitors, and some of them even as members. In 1886 the Cobden Club helped
set the tone by admitting Florence Nightingale and Mrs Cobden Sickert, Richard
Cobden's daughter, to full membership; in the 1890s some other radical or artistic
men's clubs, especially the Savage, admitted women. However, the general
attitude has still been that of the Duke of Devonshire.

Associate membership is given to widows of former members who pay a
reduced subscription rate but does not entitle them to a vote at the club's annual
general meeting. One of the arguments used by opponents of allowing full
membership has been that the associate status is sufficiently generous. As one
member stated, 'Many of the lady members of the club do not want to change
the position because they only pay half the subscription rates of the male
members'. On the other hand, after the Second World War there were some
clubs which encouraged this form of membership. The Orient Club, founded
in 1824 for those who had served the Crown or the East India Company, was
losing money heavily in the early 1950s. It subsequently recruited associate
members from the wives of members and their unmarried daughters with great
success.

A rare insight into the different treatments accorded to men and women was
provided by Jan Morris, the well known writer, who in the early 1970s decided
to change sex:

> Sometimes the arena of my ambivalence was uncomfortably small. At the
> Travellers' Club, for example, I was obviously known as a man of sorts –
> women were only allowed on the premises at all during a few hours of the
> day, and even then were hidden away as far as possible, in lesser rooms or
> alcoves … To cap this social reincarnation, I was taken to dinner at the Ladies'
> end of the Travellers' Club dining room, one of my favourite rooms.

Before the First World War, male members of upper class men's clubs who
supported the women's movement were treated with disdain. In 1912, Frederick
Pethick-Lawrence, editor of the newspaper *Votes for Women*, and then a member
of the Reform, was investigated by the club's committee after he was sent to
prison for conspiring to incite members of the Women's Social and Political
Union to damage property. He was automatically expelled, and the committee
did not recommend that he be reinstated.

Change – and decay?

There have been many forces in British society in recent decades that have made change inevitable in Clubland, notwithstanding a reluctance on the part of many members. Economic pressures brought about many mergers or closures. It was calculated that there were about 120 clubs in the St James's area before the Second World War: by the 1970s the number had diminished to 40. Residential clubmen are few in number, and this has led to a subsequent loss of revenue. Multi-membership of clubs, too, on a large scale is now much rarer. With a greater appreciation of cuisine, club members have demanded higher standards of catering. Many club histories record the improvements in both food and decor resulting from the admission of women to their dining rooms. Another reason for encouraging female membership has been to increase revenue in a period when club finances have been under great pressure.

Economic change has also seen the increase of numbers of women in the professions, media and the business world. Clubs now cater for business and social functions by the hiring out of rooms. The greater educational opportunities for women has also to be taken into account, as 40 per cent of Oxbridge undergraduates are women, and they are admitted to all colleges. This has led to the admission of women to the United Oxford and Cambridge Club. Politically, too, there has been a landslide change in club membership. In the 1997 Blair cabinet, only three members declared a club affiliation, and none was in the main league. Gavin Strang, Transport Minister, was a member of two miners' welfare clubs; Frank Dobson, Minister of Health, was a member of the Covent Garden Association; and Tony Blair was a member of his constituency's Trimdon Working Men's Club.

Clubs have come up with different solutions to the vexed question of mixed membership. The London Diary of *The Times* reported on the 22 April 1980, 'There is a dangerous whiff of revolution in the air of the Reform Club'. Sir Alan Neale, a former Permanent Secretary at the Ministry of Agriculture, Fisheries and Food, as chairman had raised the deeply contentious issue of admitting women to full membership. Two previous attempts, the last one eight years earlier, were so bitterly opposed that it was rumoured that 'chauvinism will once again win the day, even though the club treasurer could well do with those extra women's subscriptions'. The paper reminded readers that it was at the Reform Club in the film version of Jules Verne's *Round the World in 80 Days* that Phileas Fogg announced his circuit of the world, with the veteran actor Finlay Currie exclaiming, 'Great Caesar's ghost, a woman in the Club!'.

Subsequently, members voted two to one in favour of opening membership to both sexes, but the recommendation was turned down at the annual general meeting. Opponents claimed that many would resign, and 'takings would go down and new toilets would have to go up'. Supporters on the other hand pointed out that a club calling itself Reform really ought to live up to its name. After more prolonged discussions, at the end of May 1981, the club agreed to admit women for the first time in its 145 year history. Nine were nominated and were to be interviewed by the Club's Committee before an election could take place. They included a novelist, a Commissioner of Income Tax, a public relations director, and a Social Democratic Party organiser. One told a reporter, 'I am not a clubbable person, I am 45 and rather thought of my grandchildren and how it might affect their lives. It's a bit like Everest. I did it because it's there'.

A very different picture emerges when the question of voting on the admission of women members surfaced at the Carlton Club in 1998. The members were asked if they would give the 72 associate members full access to its facilities, including voting at the annual general meeting. The then Conservative Party leader, William Hague, urged MPs and party workers to follow his lead and support the change. There had been a precedent for such a move. The club had decided in 1974 that, in the event of Margaret Thatcher beating Edward Heath in the election for Party leader, it was happy to break with tradition and invite her to become an honorary member of the club. When she was successful, she accepted, and in the words of the club's historian, 'It was an honour for both her and the Club'.

Following Hague's plea, a vote in favour of allowing women to become full members was passed on 19 May 1998 by 108 to 92, but fell short of the necessary two-thirds majority. The leader now threatened to resign from the club, a move which had no precedent. However, a further snub was administered by the members in October when at an extraordinary general meeting on the same issue the motion was carried by 125 to 96 votes, thus failing once more to secure a majority. One member, Sir Rhodes Boyson, a former Conservative Education Minister, commented, 'Mr. Hague is a free man and the Conservatives are free men, thank God. We are not like socialists. We have the independence of our minds'. A more acerbic response was from the colourful Conservative MP, Teresa Gorman:

> I don't give a stuff whether Mr. Hague belongs or doesn't. I wouldn't dream of joining a gentlemen's club. They are dingy places, stuffed with the most ludicrous old men. The Conservative Establishment has always treated women as nannies, grannies and fannies, not as intelligent, equal contributors to society'.

When the matter was again raised in November 2000, out of the club's 1,550 members only 166 voted in favour of changing the rules. Although some members, including two former front benchers, resigned in protest, as late as April 2001, Hague did not act, being reported as saying that the issue was not high on his agenda. When later that year Ian Duncan Smith succeeded Hague, he caused a stir by refusing to join the Carlton because of its attitude towards women members:

> As the leader of the Conservative Party that believes there should be no 'no-go' areas for women, I will have to say that I can't do it. I'm not going to

make any demands. I personally hope the club does take women, but it's up to them.

The chairman of the club's political committee responded to this by saying, 'I am more than surprised, particularly when in fact the club made donations in the last Parliament of nearly one million pounds to the Conservative Party'. He added, 'I would have thought Mr Duncan Smith would have wanted that to continue'. Theresa May, the only lady associate club member in the Shadow Cabinet, resigned in protest, but defended her leader's decision to remain a member of the all-male Beefsteak Club.

This of course raises the question: if they are as dreary as Teresa Gorman claims, why would women want to join these élite men's clubs, where they would in any case be unwelcome? A major reason has been in the past, and still is to some extent, that these are places where important decisions are taken informally and quietly. Exclusion from the Carlton Club, for example, means in effect that one is excluded from the high councils of the Conservative Party, or at least from sources of rumour and general unofficial sources of information. In other clubs members might find themselves in company with men who had influence in financial and industrial circles. So membership of these gentlemen's clubs confers certain major social privileges, and to a certain extent it can be said that excluding women as women is depriving them of their right to enjoy these privileges if they fulfil other criteria.

Legislative attempts to change the exclusion of women from clubs have not been cordially received by successive governments, even in the twenty-first century. One campaigner, Robert Walter, Conservative MP for Dorset North, resigned from the Carlton after his future wife, a Tory candidate in the 1997 election, was stopped from entering the bar of a golf club where she was to give a speech. Walter made several efforts in Parliament to introduce a Sex Discrimination (Amendment) Bill, and at the Carlton annual general meeting in 1999 raised the matter again. He subsequently told the Commons, 'After the meeting otherwise intelligent men told me I should have been asked to resign on the spot for having the audacity to ask the Committee to reconsider its decision'. In December of the same year he was fortunate enough to draw number 11 in the private members' ballot. Walter's Bill was 'to make provision with respect to discrimination concerning the provision of goods, facilities and access to governance by private members' clubs'. He later stated:

> If I could not change the rules of the Carlton Club, at least I could try to change the law. I was not in a high enough position to secure a decent Second Reading, but I was close enough to give my Bill an airing, if only for 32 seconds. It was, of course, blocked through the good offices of the government Whip, but not before the full magnitude of the issue had been revealed.

A further private members' bill introduced by Walter in March 2002 threatened, according to *The Times*, to put Walter 'on a collision course with Tory grandees, if passed'. Another similar measure fell by the wayside in 2004 for lack of MPs' support.

Whilst single sex clubs such as the Garrick, White's, the Beefsteak and the Carlton remain, elsewhere the hard line seems to be softening. After a ballot by members of the august Athenaeum in March 2001, 2–1 voting to admit women, the Club secretly elected 25 women to join as full members in December that year. They included Susan Greenfield, a Professor of Pharmacology at Oxford University, Victoria Glendinning, the novelist, and Julia Neuberger, then Chief Executive of the King's Fund. 'They have to have some distinction', stated the former club chairman. Election procedures follow the normal course: those who knew the candidate could sign one book, and those who wished to comment on the individual candidate's achievement signed another. Six signatures were required before the candidate could be considered.

'Mixed' and non-traditional clubs

In the eighteenth century, as already noted, there were attempts to create clubs specifically designed to have mixed male-female membership. These attempts continued more or less half-heartedly throughout the nineteenth century, but left little mark. An apparent exception was the Men and Women's Club of the 1880s. This was the brainchild of the mathematician and evolutionary biologist Karl Pearson, and was intended as a serious attempt to discuss and research the relationships between the sexes, especially issues of sexuality; the women members, who included the novelist Olive Schreiner and the campaigning feminist Henrietta Müller, were generally what would later be called 'New Women'. However, the initial membership was not only tiny (six men and eight women) but selected by Pearson himself, and was less a 'club' in the usual sense than an élite discussion group. The Club represents a remarkable study in the history of sexual theory, feminism and social Darwinism, and its internal dynamics are fascinating, but its unique character is such that it gives little or no insight into sexually mixed social clubs in the nineteenth century. A much better candidate for a 'real' mixed club was reported in the *Englishwoman's Review* of April 1886. This was the Junior Denison Club, based at the Adelphi in London's West End, for

> ladies and gentlemen ... to afford to persons interested in charitable and social subjects a place of meeting and conference, a reading and writing room, and such of the ordinary conveniences of a club as may from time to time be possible.

Questions of social interest were to be discussed; annual subscription was 10s 6d, with a joining fee of 5s. There was no residential accommodation, and apparently catering was minimal. It seems to have dropped the 'Junior' at some stage, and was still active in 1904. A better known mixed club was the Emerson

Club, founded in 1911, and continuing until the late 1920s, open to both women and men, originally at Buckingham Street, The Strand, and then moving to Great George Street in Westminster. As may be deduced from its name, this was a club devoted to social reform, and 'the higher thought'; at one stage it provided an address for the Woman's Group of the Ethical Movement. Among the variety of progressive women members were the labour movement activist Clementina Black, the suffragette Myra Sadd Brown, the social purity activist Alison Neilans and the future Labour Cabinet Minister Margaret Bondfield. The third prominent mixed club of the period was the Sesame Club, founded in 1895 and still flourishing in 1916. Its name indicated openness to all, although in practice this was really a discussion and social club for intellectual women, such as the novelist May Sinclair, the campaigner Lady Betty Balfour and the suffragist-pacifist Catherine Marshall. Still, like the similar but less intellectual Bath Club and the Albemarle Club it did admit men on an equal footing with women; and although very few women's clubs went so far, as we shall see, the vast majority of them did welcome men at least as guests. In this of course they differed remarkably from their male counterparts, though in the course of the twentieth century, as noted above, most of these did at least modify their exclusion policies; and some went further. Also, new challenges have arisen.

Although many of the traditional gentlemen's clubs are changing to meet the new social and economic climate, there is now other competition in the field. There are exclusive clubs, admitting both men and women but with membership more likely to be from the arts, media, journalism and fashion. As one reporter described it:

> Today, business people have their own power networks, and the clubs that count cast their influence well beyond Pall Mall, St James or Soho. They are better organised and more commercial than the old clubs, and members are more likely to be Internet entrepreneurs than old Etonians.

A good example is the Groucho Club, founded in 1984 by two women publishers, Carmen Callil and Liz Calder, which took its title from Groucho Marx's well known jibe, 'I don't care to belong to any club that would accept me as a member'. The growth in restaurant eating is reflected in the emphasis put on the dining facilities and extensive bars in the new clubs catering for a younger age group. Moma, a club off Regent Street, offers strong national and regional cuisine and goes to great lengths to meet the demands of its members. Talking about its chefs, the club's consultant stated, 'We can't find the right chaps here. We import them from Paris'. A more unusual recent addition to London's clubs was the founding in Paddington in 2003 by Vaughan Smith of the Frontline Club, whose members are journalists working in combat zones: war correspondents, cameramen and camerawomen, and photographers. Significantly, 40 per cent of the club's members are women. Such specialised clubs are taking over from the traditional type. In an article on the older clubs as networking centres, a reporter rightly concludes, 'It is not only that the old clubs have lost members; they have lost the buzz and excitement of power, even where they retain some of its substance'.

Working men's clubs

So much for the upper reaches of society. Although insufficiently appreciated by foreigners, clubs for working-class men have been, in their way, as important an element in British civil society as the West End clubs and London-based societies aforementioned.

It may come as a surprise to those who in the twentieth century have frequented working men's clubs that the Working Men's Club and Institute Union (hereinafter CIU), the body to which most of them are affiliated, was originally established in the mid-nineteenth century by well-to-do philanthropists to keep working men off the beer. These clubs were seen as a development from the Mechanics' Institutes, which were places of formal self-improvement where working men could both acquire job-related skills and gain a broad general education. However, they only met the requirements of the highly-motivated, and it was increasingly felt that working men in general also needed a space where they could relax, meet socially and do business, and read books and newspapers – particularly a space that would provide an alternative to the pub, which in urban areas had indeed to some extent developed into the working man's club, providing a focus where the recently urbanised workers could gather informally to relax, make business and social contacts, and especially drink. By the 1850s many philanthropists, feminists, and others interested in social welfare were concerned that working men's wives and children were suffering from their menfolk's excessive consumption of beer. Although other prominent supporters of working men, such as F.D. Maurice, were involved in early attempts to provide social alternatives, the person most instrumental in setting up working men's clubs on an institutional basis was the Rev. Henry Solly, a Unitarian minister, who started the Working Men's Club and Institute Union Ltd, as it became, in 1862,

> for the purpose of helping Working Men to establish Clubs or Institutes where they can meet for conversation, business, and mental improvement, with the means of recreation and refreshment, free from intoxicating drinks; these Clubs, at the same time, constituting Societies for mutual helpfulness in various ways.

Most of the clubs referred to were actually established by wealthy, and frequently titled, philanthropists courted by Solly; to take an extreme case, the Grosvenor Working Men's Club was started by the Duke of Westminster. In addition, the Vice-Presidents and Council of the CIU consisted almost exclusively of the great and good. This soon led to tensions between the gentry who paid for the clubs and the actual members; see for example E.F. Benson's *As We Are*, which albeit belatedly gave the point of view of the landed gentry.

However, the real obstacle to the clubs' development was the lack of beer. There was a very high failure rate: of 55 clubs started in the CIU's second year, only one survived, and eventually the Council capitulated: clubs were allowed to sell beer, much to the chagrin of the Licensed Victuallers (Henry Mayhew was particularly vehement in this regard) and to the pleasure of the members, and clubs began to operate on a solid financial and social footing. By the 1880s the structure was becoming more democratic, with individual clubs more in charge of the organisation, and the 'gentry' playing a much reduced part. A degree of radicalism had become evident in many clubs, to the extent that such bodies as the London City Mission denounced them for their immorality and godlessness – understandably, since at least some clubs were taking a strong political line; for example, in 1888 the Star Radical Club in Herne Hill was committed, among other things, to Home Rule for Ireland, manhood suffrage, women's suffrage, the abolition of the House of Lords and the disestablishment of the Church of England. The tensions between the philanthropic founders and the members had become blatant. In 1889, however, the CIU was registered under the Industrial and Provident Societies Act. This meant that every club was now a shareholder in the Union, which effectively countered any attempt at domination from the centre, whether on the part of the gentry or the radicals. Another result of this seems to have been the effective de-politicisation of the clubs, which continued to increase, multiply and prosper, especially in the North of England.

By the 1920s CIU-affiliated clubs were major social centres, providing, as well as beer, books and newspapers, facilities for a wide range of pursuits, including chess, draughts, cribbage, whist, billiards, snooker and in some areas pigeon racing, and a group of clubs in the North-East had even in 1919 set up their own Federation Brewery, which became a business in its own right, eventually even supplying Parliament. Many clubs arranged social events, such as children's parties, and also began hiring professional entertainers, an activity that reached its peak in the 1960s and 1970s, when many clubs effectively became places of public entertainment attracting national and international celebrities, with club activities almost incidental, Batley being particularly remarkable in this respect. At least in the early 1970s one of the present authors remembers attending with his wife entertainment evenings at the local working men's club that included a fairly pleasant evening with a B-list, but highly professional, celebrity to be enjoyed in a leisurely fashion from one's table, with a meal and drinks. It is therefore unsurprising that by the mid-1970s working men's clubs had reached a peak from which they have only recently declined, despite the erosion of their traditional membership base of workers in heavy industry in the 1980s and 1990s, with well over 4,000 CIU clubs in Britain, and a claimed total membership of around six million. In 1977 the Silver Jubilee celebrations had included the first visit by a reigning monarch to a Working Men's Club. A century and a quarter on, the CIU had definitely arrived as a national traditional institution. Less happily, the introduction of fruit machines, and in a few cases lunchtime strippers, to some clubs in the North-East had already attracted the attentions of organised crime, which among other things inspired the cult movie *Get Carter*.

The question of who should be excluded from working men's clubs was only occasionally raised before the 1960s. The category most frequently inveighed against from the early days of the clubs was 'youths', suggesting problems of internal discipline rather than exclusion of outsiders. Conforming to notions of propriety seems sometimes to have presented problems; the female historian of the Bishop's Stortford Working Men's Club, Violet Sparrow, notes that 'the forceful language of the Bishop's Stortford working man was not noticeably affected nor subdued by threats of suspension or expulsion from the Club'. However, by the 1970s some clubs were having difficulty dealing with the demographic and social changes in Britain, and the CIU found it had inadvertently got itself into an invidious position by supporting a club which was not even a CIU affiliate over an issue of racial discrimination, when the House of Lords ruled that the East Ham South Conservative Club was exempt from the provisions of the 1968 Race Relations Act since it operated 'a genuine system of personal selection of members'. At the time the CIU took its stand on the autonomy of individual clubs to operate their own rules on the principle of privacy. However, the situation was exacerbated when the Lords extended their ruling to apply to the Preston Dockers' Club, which was operating an explicit colour bar. In 1975 the officers of the CIU found themselves summoned to the Home Office, at a time when the Home Secretary was the noted reformer Roy Jenkins, to be threatened with new legislation to cover working men's clubs, and hastened to make clear their true position by issuing a statement urging all clubs not to discriminate on grounds of race. In the late 1970s, racial exclusion was investigated and condemned by the Commission for Racial Equality in two clubs, in Edgbaston and Leeds. In the latter city a Committee Member of the Woodhouse Recreation Club was reported as saying, on seeing some Asian men looking in the Club window, which was open to the street, 'You're not coming in here, you black bastards'. Since the 1980s, despite occasional rumblings, racial issues seem to have been at worst low-key. Problems in this area derive from the highly local, not to say parochial, nature of most CIU-affiliated clubs. Club rules are frequently invoked to exclude members whose faces, according to the club committee, do not fit, and not just on grounds of race. For example, workers by brain can be discriminated against when the preference is for workers by hand. And of course Conservative Party members are unlikely to achieve easy acceptance. The bias is in favour of those who are traditionally perceived as being part of the local community, and accepting their roles therein, especially women.

The inclusion or exclusion of women has proved a more complex matter than that of race. Some clubs always have welcomed women as members, not least the Bishop's Stortford club already mentioned, which was established after a public meeting in 1873 and from a very early date had made provision for women, despite the problems of language noted above, who could attend concerts, lectures and drawing classes, and borrow books from the Library, though they were not permitted admission to the newspaper reading room until 1889. Also, from early days there was a coffee room provided for ladies, and for passing commercial travellers who were not club members. From this it can be seen that membership was not necessarily on equal terms with the men, although women do seem always to have been keen on getting admitted to club activities; for example, in Bishop's Stortford in 1906 they gained membership of the Rifle Club. Other clubs, however, have stood on the exact wording: not just 'working', but specifically 'men'. This attitude tends to be associated with the stereotypically 'backward' northern industrial areas, but can be seen as far south as Hertfordshire, where in 1943 the Bengeo Club debated the issue of opening the club to the ladies on certain nights. The resolution was defeated, but later women were 'invited to the bowling green' (in what capacity is not clear). Still, by the 1980s the only club specifically to exclude women from membership altogether was Wallsend, in the Tyneside heart of Andy Capp country. As clubs increasingly became entertainment venues, women, together with male non-members, did not suffer discrimination when buying tickets for specific events, such as hearing Eartha Kitt at Batley, especially when they paid for their own tickets. However, membership and access to other traditional club activities, such as billiards and snooker, was more problematic (see below).

Again, nationally this did not seem to be recognised as an issue until the 1970s. In the CIU, because of pressure from newly politically-conscious women (and men) the issue of women's membership was raised at the special rules revision conference in 1975, and was fully debated at the 1977 annual general meeting, when delegates rejected a motion from the Executive to entitle lady members to hold associate and pass cards, the latter allowing members to enjoy the facilities of any other CIU-affiliated club. It is interesting to note the main speakers for the motion, and their arguments. For the Executive, George Moss, President of the Union's South Yorkshire Branch, supposedly a macho stronghold, was emphatic that a rule change could bring in possibly as much as £500,000 extra funds per annum, which was an excellent reason for urging delegates to 'do away with this prejudice'. Also, Joe Wolfe of Clifton Labour Club, Blackpool, pointed out that the treasurer of their club was a woman and they had two women members on their committee. And A.W. Clifford of Silver Hall Club, North-East Branch, added that his club had had women members for the past forty years, and went on to tell the delegates bluntly:

> We are not being men if we deny women their rights. You use them to help in your clubs. I would move from our Club that women not only get Pass Cards but that they get the same rights as men. You are a little bit late in this and you have not gone far enough.

Other speakers warned the delegates that they would find themselves forced to change their rules by law if they did not do so voluntarily, but the delegates were adamant.

The big issue here was, and remains in the twenty-first century, pass cards, which, as noted above, admit members of a CIU Club to membership privileges in all CIU-affiliated clubs, and which at the time of writing are still unavailable to women, whatever the policy of an individual club may be. This is sanctioned by Rule 12(e) of the CIU: 'Associate and Pass Cards may not be issued to lady members'. Also, as late as the 1980s, examples of petty, and not so petty, discrimination were evident, usually relying on the Rule Book, or even more blatant measures. At this time there were reports of assertions that a club's annual general meeting was called off when a woman member entered. Games facilities in some clubs were declared open to children, but not to women. In at least one club a white line was painted across the floor that women were not allowed to cross. Also, in an extreme and insulting case, it was alleged that in one club a dog was not only registered as a member, but given the CIU pass card that women are never allowed to hold. There is a strong local tradition of hostility to women, which is supported by the perceived attitude of the centre. As Barbara Rogers put it in 1988, 'Many new "rules" invented by club committees have been aimed at the women who win snooker matches against the men, and have suddenly found themselves excluded from practising or playing in the club leagues'. She refers particularly to the case of Sheila Capstick, a league-standard snooker player, who found herself being suddenly excluded from the snooker room of her club in 1978 at the point when she was obviously becoming proficient at the sport. The committee, as it appears, suddenly discovered a hitherto overlooked Rule forbidding women from playing snooker under any circumstances whatsoever. Undaunted, Sheila Capstick went on not only to found ERICCA (Equal Rights In Clubs Campaign for Action), but the Ladies' Snooker Association (motto: 'A woman's right to cues').

The problem with working men's clubs is that they have traditionally been seen as a major local centre of community entertainment, independent of gender or age, and often also of local activity. However, by the 1980s, with the decline of traditional working men's employment, especially and most severely in the CIU heartlands of Lancashire, Yorkshire and points north, CIU-clubs became increasingly dependent on the spending power of women. Again, to quote Barbara Rogers in 1988:

> Clubs literally cannot survive without women members: their subscriptions, their purchase of drinks at the bar (usually drinks with a higher profit margin than the men's beer), their bingo and use of the gaming machines, their loyalty, their very successful ladies' nights, their family outings, events for the elderly, fund-raising, and the organisation of 'ladies' committees' which are reliably reported to be more businesslike and well-supported than the male equivalents which theoretically run the clubs. 'The men are afraid we'll take over,' suggested one of the women.

Rogers also quotes an anonymous woman member as saying that the club is perceived as being safer than a pub.

The matter of pubs and women is complex. Women have usually been welcome on licensed premises provided that they were respectably escorted, i.e. by a white male, and did not actually buy their drinks at the bar, although in some severely traditional establishments (sawdust, but no spittoons) any female presence was regarded as an intrusion as late as the 1960s. Even at that date, many pubs refused to serve two women without a male in sight on the assumption that they were probably prostitutes liable at any minute to start soliciting customers. All this had changed dramatically by 1970, but even in the late 1970s the highly regarded journalists Anna Coote and Patricia Hewitt, who later became a cabinet minister in the Blair government, were refused service at El Vino, then the most popular London journalists' drinking hole, on the grounds of their sex. A legal case under the 1975 Sex Discrimination Act followed, and went right up to the Law Lords, who finally affirmed women's right to be served at the bar. As already mentioned, Barbara Rogers found as late as 1988 that women felt working men's clubs a safer space than pubs, which was not so unarguably the case by the end of the century – and this is not just a metropolitan, or even southern English, phenomenon. To cite just one example: in traditionally-minded Northumberland, literally next door to the CIU-affiliated Hexham Working Men's Club, there is a pub, part of a national chain, in the former premises of an intelligently converted 1930s cinema, that welcomes women and men not only to beer and lager and spirits at prices at least competitive with Federation Breweries, but a range of wines by the bottle or the glass, or even tea or coffee, plus a variety of meals, including nut-free and vegetarian, available from 11 a.m. to 10 p.m. In much of Britain in the twenty-first century it is finally possible for a single woman to go into a pub and order a vegetarian meal with a caffe latte without anybody raising an eyebrow.

Major sources for this chapter

A great deal has been written on West End clubs and club life, both individually and collectively. To cite just some of the general works that we have found useful: M. Griffiths: *Clubs and Clubmen*; Charles Graves: *Leather Armchairs*; Ralph Nevill: *London Clubs*; Bernard Darwin: *British Clubs*; Anthony O'Connor: *Clubland*; Anthony Lejeune: *The Gentlemen's Clubs of London*; and Tom Girtin: *The Abominable Clubman*. Just about every individual West End men's club also has its own official or unofficial history, a selection of which are to be found in the Bibliography.

Working men's clubs, though more prolific, are much less well documented. George Tremlett's *Clubmen* is an excellent historical account of CIU clubs to the 1970s. Also containing useful information are Stan Shipley's *Club Life and Socialism in mid-Victorian London* and John Taylor's *From Self-help to Glamour*. Local information and anecdotes can be found in, for example, Violet Sparrow's history of the Bishop's Stortford working men's club and Frederick Catt's history of the Bengeo Club. Rather more negative accounts are to be found not only in

Barbara Rogers' *Men Only* but in the reports of the Commission for Racial Equality.

Sources on 'mixed' clubs are scattered, and include such periodicals as the *Englishwoman's Review* and the *Englishwoman's Yearbook*. Lucy Bland has a succinct and scholarly account of the Men and Women's Club in *Banishing the Beast*. More recent information on non-traditional clubs has been taken not only from clubs' own websites, but from reports in the daily press.

3   Forces' clubs

Military clubs have traditionally been a male preserve, as women did not become members of the Armed Forces until the twentieth century. Nevertheless, the gradual admittance of women to these clubs has been an interesting phenomenon. The purpose of these clubs differed little from their civilian counterparts. A meeting called by a group of senior Army officers at The Thatched Cottage Tavern, St James's Street, on 31 May 1815 arose, in part, from 'the want of a General Military Club, permanently based in London, where officers of different ranks can have a place of meeting where they can enjoy intercourse with economy'. Known initially as the General Military Club after it was joined with the Royal Naval Club in the following year, it changed its name to the United Service Club. Eventually settling in Pall Mall, and containing a grand staircase from the demolished Carlton House, it was an immensely prestigious establishment. The game of hazard was prohibited, nor were any dice to be used, and a good library was provided for its members. The club was reputedly a particular favourite with the Duke of Wellington: the horse blocks in Waterloo Place were put there especially for him.

Ladies were admitted for the first time on 7 March 1863, but only to the first floor, to watch the procession of the Prince of Wales and Princess Alexandra of Denmark. There was a motion put forward at the 1894 annual general meeting on the possibility of admitting ladies to the coffee room for refreshments, between 4 p.m. and 6 p.m., when not needed by members, but this was defeated. In the different atmosphere of the post-First World War era, matters had moved on. The historian of the club, Major-General Sir Louis Jackson, writing in 1937, reported that there was one outstanding matter of importance to record 'which is the admission of the dominant sex in 1921'. In that year the long drawn out struggle between those who wished to be hospitable and those who did not came to an end. On 6 January 1921, 470 members assembled for an extraordinary general meeting, by far the largest attendance of any in the club's history. By a majority of three to one the club moved over to the ladies the private dining room, the card room and the best billiard room. Jackson then commented, 'Was it chivalry? Was it merely the recognition that Woman's Day had come and that it was useless to struggle? I do not know, but as an optimist I hope that what we did was well done'. This was not the first time the matter had been raised. At a pre-war meeting an admiral said that he thought it would be an excellent idea to admit ladies because 'when his wife was shopping, she could bring her parcels to the Club and wait for him'.

There were some restrictions. Lady guests were admitted by the East Entrance, and shown up to the reception room on the first floor, where they would meet up with the inviting member. Smoking was permitted in the ladies' reception rooms, cigarettes between 10 a.m. to 11 p.m., but cigars and pipes only from 8.30 p.m.; in the Ladies' Dining Room cigars were allowed from 9.15 p.m. to 10.30 p.m.

After the Second World War as with their civilian counterparts, military clubs felt the effects of the economic crisis and changing living patterns. The United Service Club was obliged to amalgamate with the Junior United Service Club in 1953 and eleven years later with the nearby Union Club on Carlton House Terrace, a civilian club set up in 1799 at the time of the attempted union of the parliaments of England and Ireland. The 1968 Rules and Regulations were more liberal minded than previously. Ladies were invited to become associates, though they were excluded from any aspects of the administration of the affairs of the club and were not entitled to attend any meetings. Qualifications for associate membership included being wives or widows of members, but had to stand for re-election. A changing room and double bedrooms were available if accompanied by husbands. Lady associate membership, which was limited to 600, was renewed annually, and the subscription was £5. For entertainment up to two tables for bridge were placed in the inner drawing room between 3 pm and 5.30 pm and 8.30 pm and 11 pm. The admission of women did not prove sufficient to save the club from its increasingly stricken finances. One more amalgamation – with the Royal Aero Club in 1971 – proved to be inadequate, and the club closed its doors five years later.

The Junior United Service Club, which has already been mentioned, has an interesting history. A number of service men, irked by the fact that the United Service Club did not admit officers of lower rank than commander in the navy and major in the army, made moves to start a club which was open to both senior and junior officers. At a meeting in 1827 at The British Coffee House, 27 Cockspur Street, a provisional committee was formed. With the aid of some senior officers, including the Duke of Wellington, the Junior United Service Club came into existence. A new building was erected in Charles Street and the club opened with a limit of 1,500 members. Although a military club, it began to allow 'strangers' on its premises in 1847 when the Club House monthly dinners were stopped and it was changed into a dining room, where a member could introduce one stranger at dinner. Until 1885, members and their guests were isolated at meals, not being allowed in the members' dining room and entry to the strangers' dining room was by a special door. From 1858, as the strangers' dining room proved to be inadequate, the north bay of the coffee room was used for eating, but was railed off from the rest of the room.

Ladies were originally forbidden to enter the club. In 1885, they were first allowed to be entertained with light refreshments between certain hours in the house dinner room and from 1892, they were permitted to take tea in the drawing room. Even this concession, probably introduced because of the potential competition from surrounding burgeoning ladies' clubs, gave cause for concern. In 1904, at the first meeting of the Club Committee, a request from a number of members that ladies having tea be allowed to smoke cigarettes was considered. The Committee's reply was a resounding 'No'. However, as in many other clubs in the late 1920s, there was increasing discussion of widening the membership. The proportion of the club 'appropriated' for their exclusive use grew. This move was not enough to keep the club, with its growing financial problems, afloat; eventually, in 1953 it amalgamated with its original senior body, the United Service Club.

The third military club to be opened, and one of the best known, was the Army and Navy Club, founded in 1837 by a group of army officers who had returned from India wishing to join one of the existing clubs but found they were already full. The Duke of Wellington, a supreme clubman himself, was again involved. He insisted that Royal Navy and Royal Marine officers should be included, and the club named the Army Club, subsequently changed to the Army and Navy Club. Membership was at first limited to 1,000, but by 1922 it had risen to 2,400. The entrance fee was 15 guineas but this was increased to 25 guineas in 1845. At first located in a building in King Street, near St James's, formerly occupied by the Oxford and Cambridge Club, it moved to a purpose built building in Pall Mall in May 1851. For many years it has been known as 'The Rag', derived from a remark made soon after the opening of the Pall Mall premises by a member, Captain William Higginson Duff. Having eaten a poor meal at the club, he called it a 'Rag and Famish affair', referring to the notorious gambling inn and the haunt of prostitutes in nearby Cranbourne Alley. The title appealed to members, some of whom formed a 'Rag and Famish' dining club. Later it was adopted as the club's nickname and shortened to 'The Rag'. It was at a club dinner in 1858 in honour of a visiting French colonel that the chairman proposed a toast, 'l'entente cordiale', apparently the first time the phrase had been used.

There were two occasions in the nineteenth century when the club admitted women. The year after the club's Pall Mall opening, on 14 September 1852, a breakfast was provided for those wishing to have a good view of the Duke of Wellington's funeral procession. The second occasion was the Golden Jubilee of Queen Victoria on 21 June 1887, when again there was a procession down the Mall. Gradually, there was a softening attitude towards the use of the building. A historian of the club, writing in 1934, asked, 'But what of the future? There are now too many Service Clubs ... New members will join those clubs which can supply the requirements of the younger generation'. The question of providing accommodation for ladies had been decided by referendum shortly after the purchase of the site. It was not until 1922 that work began on five sets of chambers, ten bed-sitting rooms, 38 bedrooms, a ladies' drawing room, and a dining room for 80. The ladies' rooms were generally considered to be the most attractive of those provided in service clubs. By 1928, the new policy was generating an annual profit of at least £500. By 1962 there were 2,859 male members and 200 lady associate members, who were either wives, widows or unmarried daughters of current members, and who paid for five years a guinea subscription. In 2004 there were approximately 6,000 members, consisting of both men and women. There are three main categories of membership: service, family and non-military friend of a service member.

Although by the early 1860s there were three major military clubs in London – the United Service, the Army and Navy, and the Junior United Service – the demand for places continued. So in 1862 three officers of the Buffs, a Royal Engineers captain and a former officer of the 17th Lancers established the Navy and Military Club, the first eventually to be located in Piccadilly. It was an immediate success, attracting 150 members, with an entrance fee which quickly rose to 40 guineas. Outgrowing its premises, it moved into 94 Piccadilly after the death of the Prime Minister, Lord Palmerston, whose home it was, in 1865. The club was generally known as the In and Out, because of the inscription on its gate posts. (There is a story that a motorist, seen leaving his car in the courtyard, when challenged by a member of staff, replied that he thought it was a car park.) In a pre-1939 reconstruction, like the Army and Navy Club, it had furnished the ladies' side with three drawing rooms, a private dining room, a private writing room, dressing rooms, bathrooms and a cocktail bar. A remarkable feature was the policy of encouraging women to become associate members. After the club's absorption of the Ladies' Carlton Club after the Second World War, their numbers increased, so that by 1964 there were 900 associate lady members. Women were allowed in the 1960s to sit in a part of the members' coffee room, even at lunch time, instead of being restricted to their own dining room upstairs. Membership has been widened to include women and sons and daughters of members. Two of the 14 directors of the club are women. The joining fee is £1,500 with concessions for different categories of membership; full members are also required to purchase at least one share in the club to the value of £2,000. The club recently moved, on selling the Piccadilly site, to 4 St James's Square, the former home of the second Viscount Astor and his wife, Nancy, and it reopened there in February 1999.

Another club which has traditionally welcomed women members is the Cavalry and Guards. Until 1976, when they amalgamated, they were very different entities. The Guards originated as a club where officers could meet who had fought in the Peninsular War against Napoleon. Founded in 1810, it was the first military club with members in London. It has had a number of different homes, the last one being in Charles Street. A ladies' annexe and a ladies' dining room were opened in 1922. In the mid-1960s there were 1,500 male members of whom 400 were serving officers, as well as 650 women members, the latter being the highest number except for that of the Navy and Military. Women members consisted of wives, widows, sisters and daughters of members. The Cavalry Club dates only from 1890. Initially founded as a proprietary club by an army officer, it became a meeting place for those of commissioned rank in Cavalry and Yeomanry Regiments, the Household Cavalry,

The Royal Green Jackets and The Royal Horse Artillery. As a club, it did not include women members, but had an enlightened admissions policy. For instance, wives of members and their children, over 17 years of age, were able to dine at the club. In its heyday, 60 débutante parties were also held there each year. Women were allowed in as guests from 1911, and they are now full members in their own right. Again, unlike many other London clubs, the Cavalry has been on its same site since it was founded, at 127 Piccadilly, though it is now shared with the Guards.

The Royal Air Force Club started life as the Royal Flying Corps Club at 13 Bruton Street in 1917. In the following year the Royal Air Force was formed, the youngest of the three services. The club initially kept its original name, but in October 1918 the first Lord Cowdray paid £250,000 for the lease of 128 Piccadilly. This had from 1904 been the home of the Lyceum Club, a distinguished venue for women involved in the arts, science, literature, journalism or music or who were university graduates, of which much more will be said in the next chapter. Lord Cowdray also gave another £100,000 to refurbish the building to enlarge and rebuild, providing many facilities for RAF officers, including residential accommodation, for husbands and wives. The splendid Piccadilly entrance was forbidden to women entering the building, with access only from the Park Lane side. As late as 1954 'a pleasant commotion' was created when it was discovered that a member of the Women's Royal Air Force, Flying Officer Jean Lennox Bird, had applied for membership and was temporarily accepted. It was only at the last second that her sex was discovered and her cheque returned with gentlemanly apologies.

After the Second World War, women were allowed to arrive at the club unaccompanied, on the understanding that they would be met by a member. A ladies' lounge was provided and a bar at which the sexes could mingle. Since the early 1980s, membership of the club has been open to all serving and former officers in the RAF and Allied Air Forces. This includes the Women's Auxiliary Air Force, the Women's Royal Auxiliary Air Force, the Women's Royal Air Force and the Princess Mary's RAF Nursing Service. Widows may apply to become full members, and full members may elect for their spouses to become associate members; this category of membership ceases on divorce or judicial separation. There are different levels of subscription for serving and formerly serving officers. The RAF Club is different from others in levying annual subscriptions for serving officers: a half of one day's pay plus VAT is deducted from their salary. In 2005 the membership was 18,500.

Brief mention must be made of two other clubs, the Victory Services and the Union Jack. The Victory Services Club at 63 Seymour Street was founded in 1907 as the Veterans' Club, with one of the co-founders being Major Rider Haggard, brother of the author. After the First World War the name of the club was changed to the Allenby Club, when Field Marshall Viscount Allenby became President. It was again changed in 1970 to the Victory Services Club when all serving members of the armed forces were admitted. Serving and ex-service men and women of all ranks can join without subscription, and accommodation is provided. Membership now stands at 38,000. The Union Jack Club at Sandall Street, near Waterloo Station, will be familiar to many people who served in the forces. It was founded in 1904 as a national memorial to the troops who fought in the South African War. It has always been open to all in the armed forces and has both residential and non-residential facilities. Ex-servicemen are also entitled to membership, provided they have served for at least two years.

So far we have been concerned with military clubs which offer a reasonably full range of amenities. There is also a vast number of military dining clubs with no premises of their own, including The Blue Seal, The Marching Knot of St Patrick, and the Fadeaways. One of the earliest was the Nulli Secundus, established by and for members of the Coldstream Guards on 4 May 1783. A limit of 14 was put on the membership, and election was by ballot. Special uniforms were worn for the monthly club dinners. Any member 'entering the state of holy matrimony' was to give a dinner. Membership on marriage became honorary, and occasioned a vacancy. The club is still flourishing; the rules have been altered, and it now has over 700 members.

Some dining clubs meet in regular club premises, such as the Cavalry Lunch Club. It consists of ex-Cavalry officers, and a 'few interlopers from Guards and Infantry Regiments' and meets twice a year for lunch, when about 40 members attend and a guest speaker is invited. It has three main purposes: to provide an opportunity for keeping members in touch, to provide advice to young recently retired Cavalry officers seeking a new career, and to help raise money for army charities. Another, the Horse Guards Club, is an exclusive club for officers, ensigns, and above, in the Dragoon Guard and the Queen's Own Hussars. By tradition, it is taboo for a member to invite infantrymen 'and may provoke challenges from his enemies for ungentlemanly conduct'. The Royal Green Jackets London Club is a more permanent luncheon club. It is open each weekday for commissioned officers in The Royal Green Jackets or any of the predecessor regiments. Membership is also open to relatives, and those with close family links to the regiment and, unlike the previous two clubs, women are welcome.

Women in the Services

One of the interesting developments during the First World War was the establishment of the three women's services. Because of the heavy casualties sustained on the Western Front in France, in December 1916 the War Office decided to accept women for duties in the armies in Britain and France in a newly-formed Women's Army Auxiliary Corps (WAAC). This move did not meet with much enthusiasm from many of the senior army staff. General Sir Douglas Haig conveyed his views to the War Office in March 1917: 'It is necessary to point out that there is a limit with regard to the extent to which replacement of unfit men by women and coloured labour can be carried out safely'. Nevertheless, the Corps attracted many volunteers to its ranks, but ceased to exist after September 1921. Seventeen years later, in 1938, two days before Neville Chamberlain flew to Munich to meet Hitler, the Auxiliary Territorial

Service (ATS) was formed. It served in many countries, especially with the British Expeditionary Force in France and in North Africa. The ATS had grown to 212,000 by 1943. In 1949, its name was changed to the Women's Royal Army Corps (WRAC), functioning until it was absorbed in 1993 into the Adjutant-General Corps. A WRAC Association was formed in 1949 which superseded the former ATS Old Comrades Association. Any woman who had served in the ATS or the WRAC was eligible to join. Its main aim has been to foster an esprit de corps, help in resettlement to civilian life and use their Benevolent Fund and work with welfare organisations for members in difficult circumstances. With its headquarters at Worthy Down, Winchester, the WRAC Association has 78 branches worldwide which offer a range of social activities. Branches are chaired by locally elected chairmen and are largely financially unsupported.

The second women's service, the Women's Royal Naval Service (WRNS), popularly known as the Wrens, was set up by the Admiralty in November 1917 to take up various shore duties hitherto performed by naval ratings. The Wrens remained an active force until it was demobilised at the end of 1919. The Association of Wrens was formed the following year. Its first president was a former head of the service, Dame Katherine Furse. Its aims were similar to those of the WRAC Association, though it included as one of its main aims 'to foster ideals of citizenship'. Examples were the promotion in 1922 of Sea Guide companies and the decision to affiliate with the Girl Guide movement. In the same year, Furse was appointed Assistant Chief Commissioner of the Girl Guides. A special feature of the Association was the annual dinner, held in different venues. In 1921, 190 members attended the meal being followed by dancing until 2.30 a.m. 'before the lights were put out'. Although the Association had no permanent premises, it was due to the initiative of an ex-Wren that an Ex-Service Women's Club was opened in London in November 1922. It was situated at 22 Courtfield Gardens, SW15 and membership was open to all who had formerly served in the women's services. There was a dining room, a smoking room, a writing room and guest rooms. Single rooms were 4/6d, a shared room for two or three, 3/6d and for four in a room, 2/6d. However, the announcement added, 'There is a large fold over screen which gives a certain amount of privacy'. Members who simply needed a place to dress before going to the theatre could hire a room for 6d per half hour; the price included a bath. The large lounge was reserved for numerous events, such as the club's regular social night and Sea Scout meetings. The House Committee included 60 per cent made up of women who had served in the ranks, and were selected by club members.

In April 1939, the Women's Royal Naval Service was revived again under its Director, Dame Vera Laughton Mathews. Although the membership of the Association was only 249, there were of 1,800 women who had volunteered for the service. With the approach of war, the latter were urged to join the Ex-Service Club at ex-service rates in order to enjoy the Club's facilities. In the year ending September 1940, when membership was no longer necessary, the club had provided 10,661 nightly beds and some 45,000 meals. The name of the club was changed to the Service Women's Club though it reverted to its original title when a new recreational centre for all ex-service women was opened by Queen Mary, the Queen Mother, in October 1949. It afforded a meeting place for annual general meetings of Old Comrades Associations as well as other activities. A big difference from the previous club was that no accommodation was provided.

The WRNS once more lost its identity as a service when it was absorbed into the Royal Navy in 1993. Nevertheless, there has been an impressive continuity in the Association of Wrens formed in 1920. Membership is open to all WRNS, Women's Royal Naval Reserve, Queen Alexandra's Royal Naval Service, the Voluntary Aid Detachment and women still serving in the Royal Navy or the Royal Naval Reserve. In 2004 it had about 8,500 members all over the world, with a third of this total being active in branches. Each branch has its own activities, which include a range of mini-reunions and social events. *The Wren*, a triennial publication, still flourishes after 84 years.

The third women's Service, the Women's Royal Air Force (WRAF), was set up by the War Cabinet in January 1918 to take over many of the duties carried out by men. It was disbanded as a force in April 1920. Dame Helen Gywnne-Vaughan, the first Commodore of the WRAF, later wrote, 'When they [the women] leave the Service, they will need, as we did, the chance to meet one another and help and encouragement in getting back to civilian life'. In the summer of 1919, a WRAF Old Comrades' Association (WRAFOCA) was established, with Gwynne-Vaughan as president. By the following year, three initiatives had been launched. A summer camp was held for former WRAF personnel, a registry had been opened for servant situations and a monthly leaflet went out to all members. By 1929 a Service Women's Benevolent Fund had been started. Subscriptions were five shillings for officers, and two shillings for other ranks. An annual general meeting was held at the 'Club' situated at 5 Buckingham Gate and successful annual dinners were held. By July 1939 when the Women's Auxiliary Air Force (WAAF) came into existence with the likelihood of war against Germany, there were 450 members. It was resolved at the 1940 annual general meeting that from April 1941, the OCA should be open to all ranks of the WAAF.

A parallel body for ex-RAF servicemen, the Comrades of the Royal Air Force Association (CRAFA), with its own journal, *The Airman*, had existed for many years. When in the summer of 1941 full military status was granted to members of the WAAF the *raison d'être* for two separate Associations ceased. Where there was both a CRAFA branch and a WRAFOCA branch, the latter was merged with the former. More importantly, on losing its separate identity in 1942, the Association dropped the word 'Women' from its title, becoming instead part of the Royal Air Force Old Comrades' Association (RAFOCA). A successor to the WRAFOCA is the Women's Auxiliary Air Force Association (WAAFA), for those who served in the WAAF between 1939 and 1949. At the latter date, the service reverted to its original title of Women's Royal Air Force (WRAF) and in 1994 was integrated into the RAF. Full membership of the WAAFA is limited to those who served between 1939 and 1949, and there is associate membership for those

WOMEN of the
ROYAL AIR FORCE
OLD COMRADES' ASSOCIATION

President ... .. Chief Controller Dame HELEN GWYNNE-VAUGHAN, G.B.E.
Vice-Presidents ... ... Chief Commandant L. M. K. PRATT BARLOW, O.B.E.
Air Commandant J. TREFUSIS FORBES.

Editor and General Secretary .   Hon. Treasurer :
MISS E. RICHARDS,   **MISS DAVENPORT,**
92, The Grove, Ealing, W.5. Tel. Ealing 1242.   64, Telford Avenue, S.W.2. Tel. Tulse Hill 3801.

VOL. 29.   JULY,—AUGUST—SEPTEMBER, 1941   No. 234

FROM OUR PRESIDENT.

I want to congratulate all old comrades who are serving, either in the W.A.A.F. or the A.T.S. on the fact that, at last, military status has been attained; they are Armed Forces of the Crown and their officers hold the King's commission. I know that those whom age or health or other duties have prevented from serving again will share our satisfaction at this great step to which we of the last war have so long looked forward. I think it came very near in 1918, but the Armistice and approaching demobilisation prevented further change. Nevertheless, every ex-member of the W.R.A.F. will be with me when I say that the ground was ploughed and the seed sown in those old days so we have a right to take pride in the harvest.

As you know I have been retired on grounds of age I will not pretend that I am not sorry, very sorry indeed, but I comfort myself with the thought that, if I were younger now, I would have been too young to be Commandant, W.R.A.F., and that I would not have missed for a great deal. Anyway I am glad to have been still in a service when the new status was approved. Remember, you who are still serving, that it carries responsibilities and a duty to do even better than before.

I am doing some work now for the Home Guard and seeing a new and very interesting side of the Service.

H. C. I. GWYNNE-VAUGHAN.

OUR PRESIDENT

By Our W.A.A.F. Vice-President
(Air-Commandant J. Trefusis-Forbes)

The last meeting of the General Committee was an historic occasion, since the President appeared with the full insignia of a major-general on her uniform. She was the first woman to be authorised to wear these badges of rank, as she had been the first to be authorised to wear those of an Air Commodore in 1918. For the second time in her life she was serving as a Chief Controller.

When, in the early weeks of 1917, our President first received the title of Chief Controller, it was approximately equal to lieutenant-colonel. She was on her way to France to command the first corps of women (apart from hospital personnel) to be formed by the Army Council. The man-power situation was serious. Many women were already employed at home as civilian subordinates; it was decided to use women in replacement of soldiers for background duties on the lines of communication in France. Serving overseas, they had to be uniformed and disciplined, so the Women's Army Auxiliary Corps (later the Queen Mary's Army Auxiliary Corps) was formed. And Mrs. Gwynne-Vaughan, as she then was, went to France to prepare for the first detachment. Under her command the corps grew to 10,000 strong; they were the first women to serve in the ranks. As we all know, the Royal Air Force was formed on the 1st of April, 1918, by the union of the Royal Flying Corps and Royal Naval Air Service. Men and women attached to flying units were transferred to the R.A.F. and W.R.A.F. Some 32,000 women passed through the ranks of the latter. At first it was not altogether a happy service; the General (later Air Vice-Marshal) Sir Sefton Brancker became Air Member for Personnel (Master-General of Personnel was the name in those days), and the Chief Controller, Q.M.A.A.C., was brought from France in September, 1918, as Commandant, W.R.A.F.

Air Vice-Marshal Brancker, in his reminiscences, summed up her work: "By the end of the year the W.R.A.F. was the best disciplined and best turned out women's organisation in the country. This remarkable achievement was due to the keenness, efficiency and sound administration of Dame Helen Gwynne-Vaughan—it was nothing to do with me, except that I gave her wide powers and all the independence that was possible."

All the same, Dame Helen has always maintained that she could have done little but for those wide powers and the ready sympathy with which her recommendations were received. She asked, and it was approved, that correspondence should be through the usual Air Force channels. She asked, and it was approved, that badges of rank should be those of the R.A.F. So she, the first woman in history, put up the badges of an air commodore, and a little later our Vice-President, Chief Commander Pratt Barlow, was the first woman to put up those of a group captain.

Peace came, the W.R.A.F. was disbanded, having left, as the Air Council stated, "a record of which it can well feel proud." Dame Helen returned to the University of London, to a professorship and a life of teaching and research. But meantime she had become President of our O.C.A. Year after year she presided at the Annual Meeting, and at the Annual Dinner, where senior Air Officers reported on the progress of the Service.

Then, in 1935, she was primarily responsible for founding Emergency Service, a private society organised to train officers in case—some day—a corps of women was needed. E.S. was recognised by the Air Council, as well as by the Army Council; it received valuable help from both. It gave to the Air Force an Air Commandant and many other officers.

Figure 3.1 Journal of *Women of the Royal Air Force Old Comrades' Association*, July–Sept 1941. The force had been disbanded in 1920.

who served from 1949 onwards. Its aims are similar to those of its 1919 predecessor. The Association issues two newsletters annually and holds reunions and an annual general meeting lasting three days in different venues, as well as an annual service in St Clement Danes, the RAF church in the Strand.

All regiments and corps of the British army have their own regimental headquarters which administer their own Associations, for example, the Queen Alexander's Royal Army Nursing Corps Association, founded in 1941, but few are large enough to warrant a dedicated club. The First Aid Nursing Yeomanry (FANY) was founded in 1907 to assist in the event of war in tending to the wounded on the battlefield. In August 1920, the *First Aid Nursing Yeomanry Gazette* reported that 'there had long been talk of a FANY Club, but we are not numerous enough to form one by ourselves'. By the end of the Second World War the role of the FANY had been expanded to service in many theatres of war, as well as providing 39 members for the Special Operations Executive. In October 1946 the FANY Regimental Club was opened at 56 Sloane Street by the Commandant-in-Chief, Princess Alice. Subsequently the club was used for annual reunions.

A movement which had its roots in war led to the setting up of service clubs. The Toc H was the brainchild of the Reverend Philip 'Tubby' Clayton, an army chaplain serving on the Western Front in the First World War. Clayton established a rest house for troops in 1915 at Poperinghe, Belgium, in memory of his brother who had been killed in action; this was known as Talbot House, and in the signals phonetic alphabet of the time its initials were 'Toc H'. The movement quickly became popular as a living demonstration of fellowship and self sacrifice, where members used their skills in all forms of personal service. In 1922, a Toc H League of Women Helpers, officially associates of Toc H, was approved by the Central Executive. Clayton saw these members as 'handmaids' rather than 'helpmeets'.

During the Second World War the Association, by then known as the Toc H Women's Association, catered particularly for women service members. A Service Club Department was opened in 1941 to supervise the cost and provision of clubs. The *Toc H Journal* in February 1943, reporting on the success of these clubs, set out in detail the needs of their users:

> The facilities which exist for service women of the day are far smaller than they are for us … It is pretty certain that women find Service conditions stranger than men and miss the atmosphere of home a good deal more … She needs more than a canteen – she wants a real club, an easy chair, a book, a piano, a place to meet her friends, a quiet room or chapel; she has special needs like a sewing-machine and a chance to wash and iron clothes.

The first club was opened at Farnham, Hampshire, and was followed by a number of others. Land Army women were also welcome, and accommodation was provided for mothers of service women in hospital. Ministry of Labour hostels for munition workers were also staffed by Association members. In 1943 a Married Couples' Service Club was opened in Kensington, which also catered for single women. It was well patronised but was destroyed in the London Blitz in the following year. Most of the clubs closed down at the end of the war and the Association concentrated its energies on work overseas. Although all three main branches of the armed forces now consist of men and women, the fact that the latter are still excluded from front line combat duties such as are carried out by infantry and armoured regiments or by those manning strike aircraft still makes for differentiation in regiments and some clubs.

Major sources for this chapter

In addition to reports and periodicals of the various clubs and associations, the following have been found useful: Cordell W. Firebrace on *The Army and Navy Club*; C. Graves' *Leather Armchairs*; and A.H. Firth's *The Junior: A History of the Junior United Service Club, 1827–1929*. *Women of the RAFOCA* also contains interesting information.

FANY in particular has generated an extensive literature, including: H. Popham's *FANY: the Story of the Women's Transport Service; First Aid Nursing Yeomanry Gazette*; and Irene Ward *FANY Invicta*.

Special use has been made of material at the Imperial War Museum, such as *The Wren, WAAF Association News, The Women's Transport Service Gazette* and the publications of the WRAF Old Comrades' Association.

4 Women's clubs

In 1869 an anonymous writer in *Tinsley's Magazine* noticed a nascent movement towards social clubs specifically for women, possibly inspired by the establishment of the Working Women's Club in London, of which more below. He was incredulous and dismissive of the mere idea:

> The women who want to shut themselves off entirely from male society have already plenty of means of doing so. It is not a club they want, but a convent. And if they object to sisterhoods of all kinds, they may spend their days in the entomological rooms of the British Museum, where no man of woman born is likely to speak to them.

Later, the anti-feminist journalist and novelist Eliza Lynn Linton unsurprisingly castigated women's clubs of the 1890s in her novel *The New Woman in Haste and at Leisure* as 'a nursery for man-haters and rebels, and the nucleus of the new order of feminine supremacy'. In sober fact, however, hardly any women's clubs completely excluded men from the premises: at the minimum, men were usually welcome as invited guests of members, and were most definitely employed as servants. In the 1890s the only London women's club explicitly to forbid access to males over seven years old 'save for the porters and footmen' was the very socially exclusive Alexandra Club, whose principles of exclusion were not limited to the male sex; it was only for ladies eligible to attend the Queen's Drawing Rooms, which presumably meant that divorcées were unwelcome – and this would also definitely have applied to women of slender means, who could not in any case afford the subscription. Indeed, a few women's clubs, most notably the Ladies' County Club and the Empress Club, were actually started by men.

Despite all this, man-hatred was a usual slander levelled at all women's clubs, especially at those with progressive principles. It was often maliciously rumoured that the Pioneer Club, which was probably Linton's principal target, had a sign on its door to the effect that gentlemen and dogs were not allowed beyond the vestibule. However, the truth is that even that doughty feminist body not only permitted men as guests, but specifically invited them as speakers; also, although members were only allowed to bring the same guest to one event a month, an exception to this rule was made in favour of husbands. Similarly, the very smart

Green Park Club invited members to bring a gentleman guest to their weekly concerts free, while a woman guest would be charged five shillings; and when the journalist Hulda Friederichs called at the Pioneer Club in 1896 to interview its President, her card was of course taken up by a *man*servant. So the Pioneer Club and Green Park Club at least could scarcely be classed as 'man-hating'. Admittedly, men's access to women's club premises was always controlled, and sometimes restricted: for example, the Empress Club only allowed men into the dining room, tea room and smoking lounge, and a few clubs only allowed male visitors into one room especially reserved for the purpose. Even so, in this respect all but the most exclusive women's clubs were more inclusive than all but a very few of their male counterparts. Complete avoidance of male society was not therefore a major reason for women to have their own clubs.

So what other reasons were advanced? One obvious reason was the exclusion of women from men's clubs, leading women to set up their own equivalents. For example, the Ladies' Automobile Club was founded because of the refusal of the Royal Automobile Club to admit women members (the reason given for this was the RAC's desire to allow smoking in *all* parts of the building). Similarly, women's sporting clubs were started when men forbade women from joining the established clubs, of which more later. But there were of course other more complex motives.

In the late 1890s, at a time when women's clubs were in their heyday and were belatedly being noticed by the wider press, *Punch* claimed that the special

Figure 4.1 Drawing Room at the Pioneer Club, *Young Woman*, 1899

advantages of belonging to a ladies' club were those of meeting to talk scandal with one's neighbours, and of smoking cigarettes. This caricature is in fact somewhat closer to the mark. In all but the most austere of clubs social interaction, i.e. gossip, was an appreciated feature, and whereas a very few clubs, again like the Alexandra Club, specifically forbade smoking, many more, including the very grand Empress Club, and even the high-minded Pioneer Club, and of course the splendid Lyceum Club, actually provided smoking rooms, though even in those clubs, smoking could be a controversial issue. Still, while gossip and smoking are not to be discounted as factors contributing to clubs' popularity, they do not usually seem to have provided the initial impetus for setting up a women's, or ladies', club.

A much more important reason was connected with shopping. The earliest purely social club for women in Britain that we have identified was the Worcestershire Ladies' Club, founded in 1861 by Lady Raglan and Mrs Gregory Walkins of Woodfield, Ombersley, and situated on Foregate Street in the heart of Worcester. Its stated object was to provide a resting place, reading, writing and tea rooms for the ladies of the county on their frequent visits to the city for shopping, entertainments and general recreation. This was a pattern soon repeated in other provincial cities, notably Liverpool, Manchester and Newcastle, and eventually in Bath, Brighton, Bristol, Leeds, Edinburgh, Glasgow and Inverness; and in London one club, founded by a Mr Gilbert Oliver, quite explicitly called itself The Ladies' Tea and Shopping Club. It later became The New Ladies' County Club, described in *The Englishwoman* by Beatrice Knollys as being for women shoppers who previously had 'only the haven of some aërated bread shop, and only the refreshment of wishy-washy tea, poor coffee and poor cocoa'. Incidentally, it was also described as being convenient for bridesmaids dressing for fashionable weddings at the nearby St George's, Hanover Square. Two other examples of the club specifically for country ladies visiting London were the Victoria Club and the New Era Club, both within easy walking distance of Victoria Station.

The rise of such clubs is not surprising, given the growing importance of shopping in the social life of middle- and upper-class women in the late nineteenth century. As urbanism in general grew, such women were increasingly coming in to provincial centres, and especially to London's West End, in search of consumer goods. The presence of 'respectable' unescorted women in public space was still something of a contested issue in late nineteenth-century cities; non-prostitute women might still be importuned in Piccadilly at the end of the century, and so it was important for middle-class women (and indeed women working in the shops and related trades) to have places to go where they felt safe. Also, shopping is a tiring activity, especially when combined with travelling, and women coming into town centres needed places to recuperate, to have a cup of tea, meet their friends, and in some cases spend the night without having to pay hotel rates. And, although sources tend to be coy on this, the provision of safe, clean lavatories almost certainly increased the desirability of club membership; public lavatories for women were highly controversial at this time, since they were seen by some local councils, especially in London, as promoting

Figure 4.2 Staircase and Entrance Hall, Lyceum Club, *Ladies' Realm*, 1904

public immorality. However, department stores did eventually take notice of this need as a factor attracting custom, and in the 1890s the new Queen's Hall was the first concert hall in London to advertise 'accommodation for ladies', indicating the end of the time when, if ladies wanted to go to London, they had to be resigned to not 'going'. Also, by the 1890s, there were other places to get tea, or even a meal: the women-only Dorothy restaurants had begun operating in central London, and the tea shops of the Aërated Bread Company (ABC) and Lyons Corner Houses, though not segregating women, were beginning to provide 'safe' venues for eating out in a modest way. Additionally, as will be seen in a later chapter, in the 1880s the Young Women's Christian Association had begun doing something to help working girls by providing not only hostel accommodation but restaurants serving hot meals at low prices, at least in London. So if women's clubs had been primarily about this sort of activity, it might be expected that they would go into a decline in the 1890s.

Instead, this was the beginning of their full flowering. Writing in December 1901 a staff writer on *The Lady*, a seriously up-market magazine, noted that

> a club is now as necessary to the life of the modern gentlewoman as it has been for generations past to the man. Whether it be for the purpose of rest and quietude, intellectual debate, or for purely social motives, the woman's club is with us, and has come to stay. We see it with various objects and in a luxurious and a simple state, from the five guinea subscription club, with a stiff entrance fee, to the less pretentious middle-class club at a guinea.

The clubs which mainly attracted the attention of *The Lady* tended, of course, to fall into the former category: the Empress, the Alexandra, the Sandringham, and the Green Park Clubs, which also had a considerable, and frequently over-lapping, titled clientèle; in 1901 the Green Park Club boasted the membership of 'sisters of the King and the Kaiser'. However, at the extreme other end of the scale was the Rehearsal Club, the aim of which was 'to offer a homelike centre to minor actresses, Corps de Ballet and chorus, where they can find much needed rest and relaxation in the hours between morning and evening performances', for use of which members paid two shillings per quarter; it had no accommo-dation or restaurant, but it did have a kitchen where for a nominal charge members could bring a chop or other foodstuffs to prepare and eat. And there were many clubs in between, reflecting changing social make-up.

Alongside the development of shopping, and consequently clubs for wealthy women, there had grown up a significant body of educated professional women workers with much intellect but relatively little money, and to a considerable extent many clubs were catering for their needs. Such women also tended to live in the suburbs and travel in, and hence suffered from a degree of isolation that clubs could mitigate. In 1899, Dora Jones, writing on London women's clubs, presented a very different *raison d'être* for them:

> The modern professional woman, be she artist, journalist, clerk, doctor, teacher, or nurse, living as she often does in rooms in the suburbs, needs some fairly central haven of refuge where she can drop in, when she has a spare hour, for a rest, a cup of tea, and a glance at the newspapers.

She stresses such women's loneliness and goes so far as to claim that the club 'may stand between her and nervous breakdown, possibly even mania or suicide'. While not going so far as that, Emily Dockrell had commented the year before in *The Humanitarian*,

> What life can be more pitiably lonely than that of the cultured unmarried woman earning her daily bread hardly in London, living perhaps alone, in dingy lodgings? Picture one of them returning day after day, year in, year out, to the same atmosphere of dreary ugliness, partaking of her badly-cooked, slovenly-served, solitary meal, which she hurries through to rid herself of the hideous table appointments.

In addition, it was felt by many that women's clubs of a more intellectual and political bent would provide opportunities for women's self-improvement, as well as widening their circle of helpful acquaintances. This had always been a major impetus for the founding of American women's clubs, where the original driving force in the 1860s was 'self-culture', at first stemming from literary interests. One of the most famous examples of this was the occasion in March 1868 when the Press Club of New York held an open celebratory dinner for Charles Dickens, for which women were refused tickets. Women took various actions in response to this, but the main result was the formation in New York of the first 'Sorosis' club, not to be confused with the Soroptimists. The name 'Sorosis' is an odd choice; it is a Greek-derived technical term in botany with no obvious feminine application, but whose form does recall 'sorority' and other similar Latin-derived words. The self-culture, or self-improvement, agenda was later broadened to include philanthropy and general social awareness. Women's clubs became involved in campaigns on child labour, native American welfare, pure food and drugs, prison reform and domestic technology, among many other issues, and had a considerable impact on society; for example, in 1906 Alice Lakey, a member of the General Federation of Women's Clubs, spearheaded a letter and telegram writing campaign which is credited with securing the passage of the Pure Food and Drug Act. As Jennie Cunningham Croly, the founder of the original Sorosis in New York, put it in 1898,

> The woman's club was not an echo; it was not the mere banding together for a social and economic purpose, like the clubs of men. It became at once … a light-giving and seed-sowing centre of purely altruistic and democratic activity.

Elsewhere, she speaks of the woman's club movement representing 'a part of the great popular educational movement which is sweeping like a tidal wave over the country'. In fact, there had been 'light-seekers' organising in various states of the USA already, notably in New England and Illinois, and the movement rapidly spread not only across the USA, but internationally, especially in Australia; and in 1889 the American Dr Emma Brainerd-Ryder was instrumental in founding the Bombay Sorosis, causing a stir because of the club's lack of discrimination on grounds of nationality, caste, race or religion (although Parsis seem to have been disproportionately represented). Also in 1889, Miss Croly started the process of forming the General Federation of Women's Clubs

(GFWC), an organisation without equivalent in Britain, indicating the British clubs' relative lack of homogeneity.

The only British club that affiliated to the GFWC was, unsurprisingly, the Pioneer Club, which, according to Miss Croly, 'grew more upon the lines of clubs of women in America than most of the women's clubs in England', which were apparently seen as too much of an echo of men's clubs. The names of such institutions as the Ladies' Athenaeum and the Ladies' Army and Navy Club lent further credence to this view, and the highly utilitarian Victoria Club made no bones about the fact that it had no intellectual ambitions whatever, since it desired only 'to provide a town house for country members, and all it exacts from its members is that they should be that old-world thing, "women of no profession or calling"' (this Victoria Club is not to be confused with the Victoria League, and especially not with the Victoria Commemoration Club, which catered for nurses and other health workers). In many quarters anything else was regarded dubiously. For example, the Alexandra Club was at pains to stress that it did not go in for amusements or debates or social evenings of any kind. Indeed, Eva Anstruther's somewhat sceptical British (and upper-class) view of clubs dealing in 'self-culture' was that they effectively provided higher secondary education for the adult rich.

All the same, even in Britain, for some women at least, clubs were much more than merely a shopping convenience or a leisure facility. What they expected from clubs varied. For example, in addition to general social clubs, there were specialised organisations such as the Rehearsal Club already mentioned above, the Kennel Club, the Ladies' Dramatic Club, the Ladies' Field Club, the Ladies' Rifle Club, the Women's Advertising Club, and indeed the Writers' Club. However, there seems to have been a generally expected minimum of facilities provided both for 'town' and 'country' women. This would consist of a dining room, or at least a tea room, a dressing room, and a drawing room or reading room with newspapers, magazines, books and writing paper. A library was also welcome: the New Era Club even had an arrangement with Mudie's to provide a lending library. Good furniture and decoration were also considered important, especially by those club members whose own living accommodation was probably extremely modest. Even those clubs whose stated purpose was not social and shopping had these sorts of amenities. The Ladies' Institute, originally a women's reading room and luncheon room established in 1860 by Bessie Rayner Parkes and Barbara Bodichon, was probably the first women's club to be set up in London, and its successor, the Berners Club, started in 1869, was originally called the Working Women's Club. It was intended to provide a meeting-place for those seeking professional work or campaigning for women's education and professional employment, but despite this rather utilitarian and distinctly feminist aim even it had a dining room with meals at moderate prices, a well-equipped reading room, a conversation room and a visitors' room. Many clubs also had a room suitable for such purposes as interviewing potential staff, and some residential clubs even offered accommodation for ladies' maids, although this is less surprising taking into account, for example, Royal Holloway College's similar provision for women students in the 1890s.

As already noted, this was not peculiar to London. For example, the Liverpool Ladies' Club, founded in Bold Street in 1888 and which by 1896 was averaging 250 members, had a luncheon room, writing room, general sitting room, kitchens and dressing rooms; also 'a room which may be hired by members for interviews with servants or for committees or social gatherings'. Lunch and tea were provided, though it is unclear whether these were included in the membership fee. The club also claimed that 'all leading monthly reviews and several weekly and daily papers are taken'. In general, it was reckoned to be 'a pleasant, convenient and inexpensive resort for ladies coming in for shopping or for business'. Not wishing to be outdone by Liverpool, Manchester had its own Ladies' Club at 7 St Anne's Square; interestingly, it is noted that 'ladies visiting Manchester on special literary or public business, if residing thirty miles or more from the city, may be granted the use of the Club by the House Committee, on payment of an exceedingly moderate fee'. The Newcastle upon Tyne club, at 54 Northumberland Street, had been established in 1894, and had over 100 members. It was unusual among provincial clubs of this type in having bedrooms, as well as 'rooms where gentlemen are received as visitors'. Affiliations seem to have been important for London clubs; for example, the New Victorian Club was affiliated to the Kelvin Club, Glasgow, and to Dublin's Alexandra Club; the latter also was affiliated to the Green Park Club. In 1908 a Lyceum Club was even opened in Paris, which seems to have been regarded as an extraordinary event. As has already been mentioned in the case of Soroptimists, even in the 1920s the mere idea of a club for women in France was regarded as freakish; in 1908 it must have seemed unprecedented. This is possibly because the concept of women's clubs harked back to the much-derided feminist attempts associated with the risings of 1848. Still, leaving aside the international aspect for the present, there were almost certainly other women's clubs in provincial centres as early as the 1890s whose existence we have not yet established; and we have not yet been able to ascertain details of fees or subscriptions even of those we have found.

The above, then, give some idea of the basic facilities club members might expect for their subscriptions. Some clubs went much further: for example, the very aristocratic Empress Club, and even the distinctly less smart New County Club (successor to the Tea and Shopping Club) and the Grosvenor Crescent Club (a development of the Pioneer Club) by 1900 not only had a telephone, but actually an exchange telegraph, providing stock market reports on tickertape for members' use, which reflects élite men's clubs of the period (it will be recollected that even Soames Forsyte, 'one of the least of club-men', repaired to his club on 1 August 1914 because he 'had a sudden longing for telegraphic tape'). A number of clubs provided sporting facilities: at the height of the cycling boom the Green Park Club had its own cycling enclosure at Battersea Park, the New Victorian Club had golfing links with St Andrews, and the Sandringham Club had a special Golf Committee, with arrangements to play at the Romford

Golf Club from November to May. Billiards was also popular. Rather less energetically, the Sandringham Club boasted a winter garden where members and their friends, including men, could 'chat and have tea and cigarettes', as well as a French chef. Some of the more expensive clubs provided an 'orchestra', which does not seem to have meant a 90–player symphony orchestra, and in some clubs, perhaps less misleadingly, it was called a 'band'. More specialist clubs had appropriate 'extras': for example, the 'social and musical' Green Park Club held musical and dramatic entertainments on alternate Fridays during spring, summer and winter, in which artistes as distinguished as the composer Maude Valérie White and the dramatist Henry Beerbohm Tree participated.

In fact many clubs laid on social and artistic events of this type, which shaded easily into the self-improvement category. Lectures, discussions and debates proliferated. The more intellectually-inclined clubs especially held frequent events of this type, covering a wide range of subjects. The Somerville Club, dating from 1878, was in fact almost exclusively devoted to discussions and lectures and similar manifestations of 'self-culture', and other clubs with a wider remit also regularly organised them. For example, during the 1890s the Pioneer Club, probably the leader in this area, held talks and discussions on such topics as codes of honour, the ethics of imprisonment, the financing of voluntary schools, Ibsen's *The Master Builder*, clairvoyance, the position of women in the New Japan, the effect on the brain of street noises, theosophy, the nature of sanity, Wagner, the conflict between marriage and career, and an apology for tramps. There was even a lecture by the headmaster of Harrow School. The theoretically mixed-sex Sesame Club, mentioned in Chapter 2, had a similar programme of discussions and lectures, also including Ibsen (essential for the New Woman); and in addition to Ibsen, the New Victorian Club had weekly lectures on such themes as 'The Polite and Impolite Writer', physical culture for women and the question 'Why does the present age shirk domestic life?'. Debates were organised, although apparently on a relatively informal level; and later on the equally intellectual, albeit plusher and more sybaritic, Lyceum Club also held debates, of a more formal 'Oxford Union' type. To cite some sample motions at the Lyceum Club from 1920: 'That the Turk should be compelled to leave Europe'; 'That it is desirable that England, as well as America, should go dry' (the proposition was resoundingly defeated); and 'That autobiographical self-revelation is justifiable'. The Lyceum Club, incidentally, also held weekly dances. Unfortunately, there seems to be no record of the comparative attendance figures for these events, which might have been revealing. It certainly was in the case of Women's Institutes, as noted in Chapter 7, where turnout for purely social events, when recorded, seems often to have been well in excess of that for more demanding talks and discussions. Other clubs that in the 1890s provided intellectual fare for their members, usually of slender means, included the New Somerville Club, whose premises were originally and aptly above an Oxford Street ABC restaurant, and the Camelot Club, which was in fact a Sunday meeting place, with no residential accommodation.

A few clubs, however, while providing little in the way of social events, specifically rejected any such intellectual stimuli as talks or debates. As the Secretary of the Writers' Club said, concerning lectures and debates, 'Our members don't want them, and they would not be attended if we had them. What they want is a place where they can rest and be quiet'. In addition the 300 members, who included many women journalists, also required somewhere free from distraction to write up their copy, and so silence was enforced in the writing room. However, even the Writers' Club was not so austere as to avoid all social events; as a commentator put it in 1899, their Friday house-teas 'have come to rank among the most interesting gatherings of literary London'. Its membership included some imposing names: the novelists Mrs Humphry Ward, Flora Annie Steel, Adeline Sergeant, Lady Jeune, and Marie Belloc Lowndes among many others. Still, it was the Club's perceived lack of social amenity, or indeed shabbiness, that led to a breakaway by a group led by Constance Smedley, who in 1903 founded the Lyceum Club, of which more later. Even more austere, as already mentioned, was the Alexandra Club; and the University Club for Ladies (now the University Women's Club) was described in *The Lady* as essentially quiet, not seeking to compete with the larger and more showy clubs and not getting involved with social events or debates of any sort. It was a 'pleasant resting-place and meeting-place', where members could also dine, lunch, take tea or spend the night.

There was one problem specific to women's clubs that is seldom mentioned: that of children. This was where 'echoes of men's clubs' was of no assistance: a notice reading 'Children and dogs to be left with parcels and umbrellas in the hall' was obviously not acceptable. Occasionally there seems to have been a suggestion of a crèche, but this never appears to have been put into practice, and in fact children generally seem to have been excluded altogether – an apparently anomalous situation that can be found in certain pro-women establishments even in the early twenty-first century. This is in marked contrast with the attitude of many Women's Institutes, as will be dealt with in more detail below. Nevertheless, it may be that many clubwomen were actually happy to escape, however briefly, from the demands of child care, and were glad to have an excuse not to take the children, their own or other people's, with them.

The membership, the premises, and to some extent the activities, of clubs were determined by considerations of money and class. At the upper end were such clubs, already mentioned, as the Alexandra and the Empress, whose finances were managed by a committee of aristocratic ladies. The Empress in particular was luxurious, and at one stage its Dover Street premises seemed more to resemble an extremely well-appointed and exclusive hotel: it had 70 bedrooms, as well as sitting rooms in Louis Quinze and Venetian styles, and on the stairs there were stained glass windows depicting Shakespeare heroines. In 1901 members at dinner in the Georgian style dining room were regaled by 'orchestral music proceeding from a grille above the entrance'. The New County and Green Park Clubs also boasted 'orchestras', while the Grosvenor Crescent merely made do with a 'band', which played twice a week during meals. In the early 1900s the

Empress Club's entrance fee was ten guineas and the subsequent annual subscription was three guineas; the Alexandra at five guineas, cost less to enter, but had a higher subscription level: five guineas for town members, and four for country members. Exclusivity was not merely a matter of finance. The Alexandra Club and the Green Park Club, among others, limited membership to ladies eligible to attend the Queen's Garden Parties (hence, presumably, excluding wealthy divorcées, among very many others). There was no shortage of candidates to join; the Empress had an upper limit to membership of 3,000, and by 1899 had refused admittance to half that number again.

A rather different picture was presented by the Lyceum Club which, although also very well-appointed, was by no means as socially exclusive as these. It was open to women of any nationality who had either published any original work in literature, journalism, science, art or music, or had university degrees; 'social members' who had none of these qualifications could also join, though at a higher subscription rate. As already noted, it had been founded in 1903 by Constance Smedley, who was herself from a wealthy background, on the assumption that professional women, especially writers and journalists, required 'a substantial and dignified milieu where they could meet editors and other employers and discuss matters as men did in professional clubs: above all in surroundings that did not suggest poverty'. The club certainly achieved that. As Dora D'Espaigne remarked in the *Lady's Realm* in 1904, its original premises were perceived as a physical encroachment on élite men's space. 'A ladies' club in Piccadilly!' This was not really as much of an encroachment as it might seem, since many of the wealthier women's clubs, such as the Empress, the New Century and the Sandringham, were near by. However, a significant border had been crossed.

The Lyceum Club was initially housed at 128 Piccadilly, in premises which formerly belonged to the Imperial Club, and now are the home of the RAF Club. This was an accommodation that in no way suggested poverty, but even that was outshone when in 1919 the Lyceum Club moved to 138 Piccadilly, a splendid house whose 'decorations include a *chef d'œuvre* of the Adam Brothers and paintings reputed to be by Angelica Kauffmann in the ceiling and panels respectively of the Dining Room'; however, as we shall see later, this was not a particularly wise move. Members initially numbered 1,000, and in 1909 the subscription and entrance rates were: town (i.e. London), four guineas, entrance fee, two guineas; country, three guineas, entrance fee, one guinea. Its members were arranged in 'sections': Agriculturalists and Horticulturists; Authors; Arts and Crafts; Dramatists; Geographical; Journalists; Music; Painters; Photographers; Public Service; Social; and University. Most activities were arranged in 'Circles', which would be addressed by 'lecturers of repute and experience'. By 1920 the Circles comprised: American, Belgium [sic], French, Irish, Italian, Oriental, Polish, Russian, Scottish, United Empire, Art Lovers, Geographical, Music, Photographers, Poetry, Billiards, Bridge, and Psychic. A major general activity was the Club's Monday House Dinners, with eminent after-dinner speakers, at which 'the most celebrated representatives of the arts, and the Ambassadors and Embassies of various countries' were entertained. Special features of the club included an art gallery, where exhibitions of highest standing of members' work was on view; monthly concerts, when original compositions were performed by distinguished artists; and a book gallery, where members' books were sold. There was also a Bureau which 'renders services in many ways to professional members'. Initially there were 35 bedrooms. It had considerable international influence. Soon there were Lyceum Clubs in Amsterdam, Athens, Basel, Berlin, Berne, Barbados, Brussels, Florence, Geneva, Hobart, Lausanne, Madrid, Melbourne, Milan, Nice, Paris, Rome, Stockholm and Sydney. In the 1920s the Florence Lyceum appears to have been particularly active; in 1928, for example, it was addressed by the Futurist and Fascist supporter Emilio Marinetti, though it should also be noted that this professional misogynist had already spoken at the London Lyceum Club in 1910, shortly after the unveiling of the Futurist Manifesto.

The Lyceum Club's membership also included many distinguished names: its first chairman was Lady Frances Balfour, who was succeeded, some time prior to 1920, by Lady Aberdeen; her vice-chairman was Enid Moberly Bell, and the first honorary secretary was Constance Smedley. Other high-profile women included the Mistress of Girton, the headmistress of Roedean, Flora Shaw (Lady Lugard), the writers Sarah Grand and Beatrice Harraden, Dr Louisa Martindale, Clara Rackham (later prominent in the League of Nations), Lady Strachey, Chrystal Macmillan and the radical politician Dora Montefiore. Unsurprisingly, the Lyceum had a formidable reputation and was referred to in 1914 by T.H.S. Escott as 'this select company of modish Minervas'. In 1919 a breakaway group, led by Alice Williams, founded the Forum Club, reportedly characterising the Lyceum as too 'bluestocking', although actually the core membership came from the newly-established Women's Institutes, and the activities of its WI section were reported in the WI monthly *Home and Country*.

Although the members would probably have regarded such terms as 'self-improvement' or 'self-culture' with great scepticism, the Lyceum Club in many ways provides a link between the élite women's clubs and those of a more political and intellectual nature. There were indeed various clubs of that type, including for example the Halcyon Club, apparently founded in 1914, that tended to go for high thinking and plain living. However, the most illustrious of the intellectual and reforming clubs was definitely the aforementioned Pioneer Club. It was established in 1892 by Mrs Emily H. Massingberd, of Gunby Hall, in Lincolnshire, now a National Trust property. She was a leading social worker and proponent of temperance; she had bought a local pub and abolished the sale of beer (it is now called 'The Tastee Lamb', and sells lamb and eggs). Beatrice Knollys in the *Englishwoman* in 1895 noted that she was 'one of the few women entitled to wear a crest'. It will therefore come as no surprise to learn that she also had considerable private means. She was definitely regarded as the founder of the Pioneer Club, and was referred to in club reports as 'the President'. Hulda Friederichs in the *Young Woman* in 1896 noted that she looked rather like the famous, not to say notorious, proponent of birth control, socialism and theosophy

Annie Besant, and it would appear that both these women shared many concerns, not least that of progressive education, and what came to be known as the Higher Thought. She subsidised the club considerably until her untimely death in 1897, and indeed it never really attained the sort of financial independence she wished for it.

In the 1890s members of the Pioneer Club had the reputation of being 'of all the new women and shrieking sisters the newest and the loudest; man-hating, but mannish in their dress; and woman's-righters, without a single right notion in their heads', as Hulda Friederichs put it somewhat ironically. This was of course a caricature, but there were elements of truth in it. Members of the Pioneer Club were certainly 'woman's-righters', since most of them campaigned vigorously for women's property rights, the reform of marital law and, most radically, giving women the vote. It was sometimes claimed that evening attire for members consisted of a black satin jacket, white collar and tie rather than more conventional dresses, but judging from contemporary photographs, this may have reflected more the habitual dress of a minority of the members (including, be it said, the President); most Pioneers seem to have dressed relatively conventionally. In 1895 Beatrice Knollys noted that divided skirts, short hair and 'manly costumes' were only worn by relatively few women. Members stoutly denied man-hating, pointing to the number of men they invited as speakers. Nonetheless, its reputation for progressive ideas was well merited. Theosophists, campaigners for vegetarianism and against vivisection, temperance campaigners, internationalists, socialists and others of a generally 'radical' or 'progressive' frame of mind felt at home there. In the 1890s it almost seemed that in order to be thought a 'New Woman' you had to be a member of the Pioneer Club.

The Pioneer Club was portrayed as a place where women gathered 'to meet each other, to help each other and to discuss the leading questions and principal progressive work of the day', as it was reported in 1893 in *Shafts*, the progressive feminist periodical conducted by Margaret Shurmer Sibthorpe, which gave extensive accounts of the club's activities until the demise of *Shafts* in 1899. The club's name was a conscious reference to Walt Whitman, the relevant quotation being on a glass screen in the hall:

> We the route for travel clearing
> Pioneers, O Pioneers!
> All the hands of comrades clasping
> Pioneers, O Pioneers!

Other quotations from Whitman were displayed elsewhere on the premises, and in 1897 a Frederic Remington sculpture of a 'Pioneer Woman' was presented to the Club. It was open to all classes of society who were united in the common cause of doing good works, and was strongly associated with 'the higher thought' as well as such associated issues of the 'New Morality' of the late nineteenth century as the previously indicated theosophy, but also anti-vivisection, anti-vaccination and above all feminism. Activities, which were suspended during August and September, included, as already mentioned, talks and debates on topical issues, with such speakers as George Bernard Shaw, Millicent Fawcett, Mrs Pearsall Smith, Lady Henry Somerset and Frances Willard. There were also dramatic readings, recitals, recitations, concerts, etc. These activities were reported in various places, but most consistently and most fully in *Shafts*, whose editor, Margaret Shurmer Sibthorpe, was a prominent member. Other members included the socialist Eleanor Marx Aveling (daughter of Karl), the writer Olive Schreiner, the above-mentioned radical Dora Montefiore, the novelists Sarah Grand and Mona Caird, and the feminist activist, editor of the *Women's Penny Paper* and the *Woman's Herald*, and theosophist, Henrietta Mueller. Interestingly, however, Annie Besant was not a member, although this is probably accounted for by the fact that she had gone to India by the time the club started. The total membership in 1893 was 320, but by 1899 had risen to over 600. The subscription fee initially was two guineas per annum, with an entrance fee of one guinea; by 1910 these rates had risen to three guineas with three guineas entrance for town members, two guineas per annum membership and two guineas entrance fee for country members. Each member wore a small silver axe, the club's badge, and was known by a number rather than by name, as a symbol of perfect equality (although Beatrice Knollys suggested that it actually recalled prisoners' numbers). It claimed to be the only temperance club in London, though, as already stated, it did notoriously provide a smoking room.

Premises were very important to Mrs Massingberd. As Dora Jones put it in *The Young Woman* in 1899,

> It was her dream to ensure that the woman who perhaps could only afford to rent a bedroom should yet have at her command something of the rest and comfort of spacious rooms, pictures, flowers, bright social intercourse and everything that pertains to a well-ordered life.

The club was first located at 180 Regent Street, London, over a perfumier's shop, where it had a drawing room and visitors' room, separated by doors that could be folded back to make one room for debates and discussions, a tea room doubling as dining room, a dressing room, and a reading room. There was also an unspecified number of bedrooms for members' use. Mottoes were displayed prominently: 'Silence is Golden' (in the reading room), 'In great things Unity, in small things Liberty, in all things Charity', 'They say – what say they? – Let them say', and most prominently, 'Love thyself last'. An allegorical painting of a female figure entitled 'The Birth of a Planet' by a Mr Maskell, a gift to the club from Mrs Massingberd, was displayed above the mantelpiece. However, Pioneers tended to stress less the club's earnest high-mindedness than its function as a refuge: a place where, as reported in *Shafts* on 3 November 1892,

> refreshments can be ordered at any time; or a lady may while away an hour, or an afternoon, of waiting in town in interesting conversation, with a friend

whom she may have appointed to meet; or in perusing some of the books, magazines or daily papers which are supplied without stint.

The Pioneer soon outgrew the modest accommodation in Regent Street and moved, first to 22 Cork Street, London, then to 22 Bruton Street, formerly the town residence of Lord Hastings. In 1897 it was due to move again to new premises at 15 Grosvenor Crescent, Hyde Park Corner, but before the move took place Mrs Massingberd died. Her death seems to have brought to a head internal dissatisfaction with the move, and a substantial proportion of the membership insisted on remaining at the original address and retaining the name of the Pioneer Club. Those who did move to the new location took the name of the Grosvenor Crescent Club, which by 1900 was declaring that its aims were 'purely social'. The Pioneer Club itself moved shortly afterwards to 5 Grafton Street, Piccadilly, then to 12 Cavendish Place, and then to 9 Park Place, London, SW. It was still active as late as 1924, but its glory days were definitely the 1890s.

An offshoot of the Pioneer Club, or rather of the Grosvenor Crescent Club, was the Women's Institute (no relation to the rural Women's Institutes discussed below). This was established by a prominent Pioneer, Leonora Wynford Philipps, in 1897. This supplemented the club's intellectual life with a library and a lecture and educational department, as well as a billiard room, but also acted as a sort of job centre, and sponsored in 1898 the landmark *Dictionary of Employments Open to Women*. The Women's Institute too seems still to have been active in the 1920s.

The 1920s also saw the foundation of another club, even more explicitly feminist than the Pioneer, the Grosvenor Crescent or the Women's Institute, this time as a late feature of the women's suffrage movement. The Minerva Club was founded at 28 Brunswick Square in London's Bloomsbury in 1920 by Dr Elizabeth Knight, a leading member of the 'moderate militant' suffrage organisation the Women's Freedom League, and a Mrs Fisher; initially at least membership of the Minerva seems to have been dependent on belonging to the League. Indeed, the League eventually took it as its headquarters in the 1950s when the lease on its own offices ran out. There had previously been an International Women's Franchise Club, but by the end of the First World War it was in financial difficulties, and closed in 1923. In 1924 Marian Reeves took over management of the Minerva Club. Here she organised many social and fund-raising activities for the Women's Freedom League, and for visitors, particularly women from overseas. Especially notable were her 'Tea and Politics Meetings', which later became 'Supper Meetings', when Parliament was in session in order to give women and men an opportunity to discuss current legislation. Marian Reeves also became something of a Bloomsbury figure, including among her friends George Bernard Shaw, Jawaharlal Nehru, E.M. Forster, Harriet Cohen, and Emmeline and Frederick Pethick Lawrence. Her hospitality to feminists of all persuasions at the Minerva Club led to her being known as 'the hostess of the women's movement'. However, at least one young woman, an undergraduate at London University, who stayed there in the 1930s, is reported by Elizabeth Crawford to have described the club as 'tatty, the carpets threadbare, and the food indifferent, although not sufficiently bad as to dissuade E.M. Forster from breakfasting there'.

Another former suffrage body, although not officially a club but a political organisation, was the London and National Society for Women's Service, formerly the London Society for Women's Suffrage, and from 1953 the Fawcett Society. In the 1930s it had many of the attributes of a club: it owned premises in Marsham Street, Westminster, with a library, a restaurant, a theatre, and a dance floor. Its Junior Council, the membership of which consisted largely of young professional women, organised a programme of meetings addressed over the years by speakers as various as Virginia Woolf and Dorothy L. Sayers. Unfortunately, the premises suffered from enemy action in 1940 and were unusable after the war. The construction of Women's Service House had already involved the society in serious debt, and in 1946 they not only had no premises but a £6,000 overdraft, which was paid off by Philippa Fawcett, the learned daughter of the suffragist leader Millicent Fawcett.

Admission to Women's Service House was restricted to members of the Society and their guests, and subscription to the Minerva Club was, as already indicated, allied to membership of the Women's Freedom League. However, subscription rates and club finances in general present a complex picture. Although in the 1890s rates at the Pioneer Club had been lower than that of other clubs mentioned at that time, in an era when an above-poverty family wage was reckoned to be 'Round about a Pound A Week', as Maude Pember Reeves entitled her study of working-class life in 1913, it was not cheap, and this factor did limit membership. Few working-class women belonged to a social or political club of this nature; the very cheap Bee Club and the Beechwood Club in Chelsea were more likely to have catered for impecunious 'bohemian' artists and writers than to factory girls or washerwomen. Finance was in fact a constant problem for all but the richest clubs, and many even of those were in fact subsidised heavily, like the Pioneer in its early palmy days. In 1869 the Working Women's (Berners) Club had started out with a subscription of five shillings, but this rapidly had to be doubled, and in any case this was largely nominal: the club depended on subsidy from wealthier members. Women have always tended to have less disposable income than men, and this was particularly the case in the late nineteenth and early twentieth centuries. Clubs supported entirely by membership subscription were rare in the extreme. One such was the Somerville Club, whose demise in 1900 prompted the *Englishwoman's Review* to note that the only remaining women's club actually owned by the members was the Writers' Club, the somewhat spartan nature of whose premises has already been noted (in 1900 they were accommodated in a semi-basement).

By this time the more usual way of financing a club was to make it 'proprietary', i.e. to set up a separate company, or more rarely a trust, whose function was to carry on the business of the club. We have already seen such companies in the case of the Alexandra and Empress Clubs, the latter being established by a Mr Otto Oliver, who was its secretary; and these or similar arrangements applied to other clubs as well. For example, the Sandringham Club, originally founded as the Ladies' International Club, was run by a Miss Cohen and a committee of ladies, and a Mrs Smart was not only president of the New Victorian Club, but also its proprietor. Even so, however, the few wealthy women who supported women-oriented ventures often found themselves subsidising them. There are numerous instances of this sort of subsidy, whether covert or overt, and not always uniquely by women. An overt example was the Rehearsal Club, where the members' subscription was nominal (it certainly would not even have covered the rent of the Leicester Square premises) and which effectively operated as a theatreland charity or rescue club supported by donations from the well-to-do and figures in the theatre who had made it out of their habitual poverty, including such men as Henry Irving, Beerbohm Tree and Forbes Robertson. But covert subsidy was probably even more usual, and not just of clubs. The cases of the feminist periodicals the *Woman's Signal* (1894–9) and the *Vote* (1909–33) are highly relevant. The first appeared to be an organ of the British Women's Temperance Association, but was in fact heavily subsidised by the editor, Florence Fenwick-Miller, who finally pulled the plug when her disagreements with the Association became too great; the second was even more covertly subsidised by the aforementioned Dr Elizabeth Knight, and suddenly foundered when she died intestate in an accident (the Minerva Club also suffered from her intestacy). Women's clubs were equally liable to rely on the financial support of one or two people. Miss Sarah Clegg is another figure whose sudden intestate demise in 1931 caused problems both to the London and National Society for Women's Service and to the Lyceum Club (see below for further details). In the case of the Pioneer Club we have already noted Mrs Massingberd's involvement, although after her death it seems, for a time at least, to have become a 'members' club, backed by a guarantee fund representing a majority of the membership; the Lyceum Club found its initial backing from William Thomas Smedley, father of the founder, Constance Smedley. The eventual fate of the Lyceum Club serves as a cautionary tale, and is set forth here as such in some detail to give some idea of the financial complexities that could be involved in running a club.

As already noted, in 1919 the Lyceum Club moved from its moderately sumptuous premises to extremely sumptuous leasehold ones just up the road, the road in this case being London's Piccadilly, with a rent of £3,500 per annum, with an option to purchase the remainder of the 50–year lease: dating from 1898, it had less than 20 years to run. The ground rent was £1,050 per annum and rates were about £1,200. On 15 April 1920 a meeting of first debenture holders of The Ladies' Lyceum Club Ltd, set up in 1915 to manage the business of the club, approved the purchase of the leasehold; a charge was made and a trust established to administer it, trustees being Miss Sarah Clegg and Mrs Annie Elizabeth Smedley. On 20 June 1920 the residue of the lease was purchased from Henry James King, with a down payment of £17,500, but the company defaulted when the next payment was due; Mr King obtained a judgement against the company on 17 January 1923, but the company could not comply. Sarah Clegg and William Smedley advanced the remainder (£14,121 14s 3d). Sarah Clegg had already advanced £5,000. On 31 December 1924 the leasehold premises were duly assigned to Miss Clegg and Mr Smedley. By a trust deed of 16 July 1926 the premises were held in trust for repayment of the £14,121 14s 3d plus interest and the £5,000 plus interest, by the debenture holders and the company. However, the company staggered on from year to year until Sarah Clegg suddenly died intestate in 1931, at which stage there was nobody left to pick up the bills. As already noted, the death of Sarah Clegg caused similar financial problems for the London and National Society for Women's Service, which had just taken delivery of a brand-new building which was not yet paid for. Over the period 1929–32 club expenditure had exceeded subscription income by about £6,000; William Smedley blamed for this the fact that original members continued to pay at the original subscription rate, despite nearly 30 years of subscription increases. This seems to have been normal procedure. When the Writers' Club in 1899 increased subscriptions to *all* members to cover costs of premises, it was considered to be an 'unusual arrangement'. However, when in 1933 The Ladies' Lyceum Club Ltd finally capitulated, and submitted to administration, the Official Receiver believed that the major error was in contracting to buy the freehold when the company did not actually have the money in hand to meet the cost.

The above gives some idea of what could happen to women's clubs if they did not watch their finances carefully enough. Another similar, though less drastic, fate befell the Ladies' Automobile Club in 1921, when they could not settle a bill from Heal's. However, many other clubs held off financial crisis more successfully than the Lyceum. The Empress Club did not finally close its doors until the 1950s; the New Cavendish Club, created in 1920 by Lady Ampthill to provide a meeting place for women who had served with Voluntary Aid Detachments, with premises in Great Cumberland Place, still flourishes, albeit as a mixed club; and above all the University Women's Club, established in 1886 as the University Club for Ladies, is still very active at the time of writing, and still admits men only as members of its 'Luncheon Club'. Its modestly grand premises in Audley Square, in the heart of London's Mayfair (Dorothy L. Sayers mischievously made Lord Peter Wimsey reside there after his marriage), continue to give an impression of the atmosphere of a women's club a century ago. It has residential accommodation, a dining-room with excellent catering, bar facilities for members, a well-stocked library and an elegant drawing room. As well as their use by members, the library and drawing room are often hired out to the media, as for example in the classic BBC Miss Marple episodes, in some of which those who know the club will recognise the general décor. It also hires out rooms for meetings, especially of organisations which no longer have their own premises, such as the International Lyceum Club of London, successor to the magnificent but extravagant institution whose fate has been described above. To digress briefly on the later history of the Lyceum Club: for a while it seems to have become a sort of subset of the Forum Club, but in 1964 it re-established itself as an independent entity, albeit on a much more modest scale. Meanwhile, Lyceum Clubs throughout the world continue to flourish, especially in Australia; it seems to be only in London where the Lyceum's existence is problematic.

Other clubs have coped by changing themselves. The Sloane Club, which was originally the Service Women's Club, continues as a purely social facility, but without a forces link, admitting men to membership, and a few other commercial clubs attract similar custom. Still, the Sloane Club does at least host weekly morning lectures: according to *The Times*, in 2002 subjects included 'great British food finds', authority dressing, the lowdown on HRT, and a talk on matrimonial law by a Mayfair law firm which also offered members divorce advice for £5.00 (£10.00 to non-members). The very exclusive (and expensive) Lansdowne Club is a relative newcomer, and prospers in a discreetly opulent way. On a more modest level, the National Association of Women's Clubs represents a network of groups that meet occasionally in hired rooms or halls for talks or social get-togethers. So women's clubs are far from extinct. Generally, however, traditional women's clubs appear to have had their heyday, and finance has probably been the major factor in the disappearance of so many of them; the survivors as well as the new clubs are not cheap to join. However, at the time of writing there does not generally seem to be the same perceived need for clubs specifically for women as there was in the early twentieth century. Women in Britain in the early twenty-first century by and large appear to find enough spaces to enjoy a varied social life, and relatively few of them feel the need for women-only space of the social club type.

To sum up: women's clubs have above all been an attempt to claim social and physical space for women especially in city centres. In the case of the wealthier clubs, this was mainly just claiming equality with their menfolk, but they nevertheless made it possible for less well-off middle-class and professional women on their own in major urban centres to have the sort of social base for activities that could otherwise have exposed them to risk. They helped considerably to establish women's right to be in the city. They also provided a haven for middle-class women from the demands of family, children, servants and tradesmen and even, as Virginia Woolf put it, rooms of their own. They have also helped with networking; like-minded women have been able to communicate in a way that men have always taken for granted. Above all, they have given women a space, however limited, in which to enjoy themselves.

Major sources for this chapter

Sources here are multifarious and highly dispersed. An excellent secondary source for the general context of late nineteenth and very early twentieth century women's social clubs in London is Erika Rappaport's brilliant *Shopping for Pleasure*, which is in any case highly recommendable to anybody interested in women's social history. A good account of the situation in the 1890s is to be found in David Rubinstein's *Before the Suffragettes*. Apart from that, for the period before 1920, there are various articles in contemporary periodicals, such as the *Englishwoman*, the *Englishwoman's Review*, the *Englishwoman's Yearbook*, the *Humanitarian*, the *Lady's Realm*, the *Nineteenth Century*, *Shafts* and the *Young Woman*. Constance Smedley gives an account of the beginnings of the Lyceum

Club in *Crusaders*. Annual reports and club journals do exist, but are extremely hard to come by. Information on the financial situation of the Ladies' Automobile Club, the Pioneer Club and especially the Lyceum Club are available at the National Archive at Kew.

5 Sporting clubs

The early context

The issue of women and sport is as much a contested area as that of women in public places. Although lower-class women had little opportunity to avoid the healthy exertion involved in hard work, it was only reluctantly conceded that women of the wealthier classes might benefit from some exercise. Millamant, the heroine of Congreve's *Way of the World*, produced in 1700, notoriously expressed the fashionable lady's disdain for even simple exercise because of its vulgarity: 'I nauseate walking, 'tis a country diversion'. Still, women did sometimes take part in vigorous activity, particularly dancing and riding, and by the mid-nineteenth century a general concern for women's physical health was gaining ground. This was partly due to feminist persuasion, especially campaigns around dress, beginning with protests against the crinoline skirt (among other things, it was a real fire hazard) and tightly laced corsets, and developing into the movement for rational dress as pioneered by the American Amelia Bloomer among others. However, eugenic considerations also played a part; Herbert Spencer was one of many men at this time who saw a necessity for healthy, physically fit mothers to breed a healthy race. This was not as straightforward as it might seem, since there was plenty of opposition to women's vigorous exercise on the grounds that it 'masculinised' the women who undertook it, and therefore reduced their eugenic potential. As late as 1920 the eugenist Arabella Kenealy was asserting that playing hockey incapacitated women for lactation. Also influential was the idea of the expenditure of energy as a zero-sum exercise – the more energy you used, the less you had left for such necessary activities as childbearing.

Even so, by the early nineteenth century, if not earlier, young women at least were encouraged to undertake some minimal exercise. Such publications as *Heath's Book of Beauty* in the 1830s recommended easy exercises with Indian clubs, and sedate walking was systematically practised by girls' schools: the organised walk in a 'crocodile' was an inescapable feature of girls' school life well into the twentieth century. Correct posture was increasingly seen to be desirable, partly for aesthetic reasons, but also to improve girls' health, and to this end there was an increasing interest in callisthenics. At first this involved little more than the Indian clubs and elegant walking already mentioned, but eventually girls' schools began to follow the practice of boys' schools. The main impetus as regards boys' physical education was initially military, because of concern over the generally poor health of army recruits, and military style drill had been introduced as part of many schools' curriculum; and girls followed suit. So before long the drill sergeant was also a feature of girls' schools. This militaristic system was soon superseded. In Sweden, Per Ling had established a completely different system of gymnastics, based on therapeutic principles, and it was not long before the influence of this spread to Britain. The London School Board in 1879 appointed the Ling pupil Concordia Löfving Superintendent of Physical Education in Girls' Schools; and in 1881 she was succeeded by another Ling pupil, Martina Bergman, later Bergman-Österberg, who became famous as a proponent of 'Swedish drill'.

At the same time, girls' schools, particularly schools affiliated to the Girls' Public Day School Trust, had been wanting to follow boys' schools in introducing organised games. However, in this respect it was probably women's higher education institutions that proved more influential, particularly the new Cambridge women's colleges. Girton began playing tennis in 1873, and established a tennis club in 1883. Despite initial fears that it might be too physically dangerous, grass hockey was started in 1890, and was soon followed by the provision of a swimming bath, a golf club, a cricket club, a lacrosse club, and of course a 'bicycling' club. Newnham College was not far behind, including fives among its sports, and in 1899 the college actually instituted carefully chaperoned mixed tennis, which marked a definite shift from the segregation that was usually imposed on women's sport. However, mixed tennis continued to be extremely unusual, and even women's participation in tennis clubs was long felt to be controversial, as will be dealt with in more detail below.

All the same, there remained a considerable sentiment against women taking part in any but the most conventional of sports. As the *Badminton Magazine* put it in 1900:

> Beauty of face and form is one of the chief essentials, but unlimited indulgence in violent outdoor sports ... especially – most odious of all games for women – hockey, cannot but have an unwomanly effect on a young girl's mind.

This prejudice against women taking part in any but the most genteel of sports was notable especially at international level. Notoriously, Pierre de Coubertin, founder of the modern Olympic Games, stated in 1902 that 'women have but one task, that of crowning the winner with garlands'. As late as 1922 the situation was little better, and the Fédération Sportive Féminine Internationale finally lost patience with the International Olympic Committee (IOC) for its refusal to include track and field competitions for women in the Olympic Games, and held the first World Women's Games. Eventually, with extreme reluctance, the IOC took the hint and included the women's events. Yet the feeling that too

Figure 5.1 Illustration from *The Graphic*, c. 1885, signed by John Jellicoe, later Admiral of the Fleet

much exertion was unladylike lingered. As will be noted, while women's golf was tolerated and even encouraged when it was restricted to putting, as soon as women started to swing and drive, that was a different matter. Vigorous activity was deemed not feminine, if not actually indelicate, as was any dress calculated to lessen the conventional constraints on women's activity.

Dress

As already seen, women's participation in sports in many ways challenged prevailing nineteenth-century concepts of femininity and female delicacy. As well as the fear of 'masculinising' women's bodies by the development of muscles in unaesthetic places, matters of dress were particularly controversial. Women were above all expected to wear long, flowing dresses or at least skirts reaching to the ground, as well as petticoats, sometimes in several layers, and by the mid-nineteenth century the weight of 'respectable' women's clothing, together with corsetry, was a serious inhibiting factor not just to women's participation in sports, but to carrying out any serious exercise. Even so, gaining acceptance for any sort of dress reform was hard going. Part of the problem was the ideology of trousers, or anything that might seem to resemble them, like 'bloomers', and resistance to this did not really die out until the mid-twentieth century. As Dorothy L. Sayers remarked as late as 1941, 'The fact is that, for [human beings], the garment is warm, convenient and decent. But in Western countries (though not in China or Mohammedan countries) [the male] has staked out a claim to it, and has invested the skirt with a sexual significance'. A woman 'wearing the trousers' even metaphorically was deemed to be subverting the dominance of the male. However, despite such feminist attitudes, at least up till 1914, most games continued to be played in long skirts. The Ladies' Hockey Association, later the All-England Women's Hockey Association, was particularly resistant to anything smacking of rational dress or indelicacy, despite the fact that playing hockey in long skirts effectively hindered women from playing hockey on equal terms with men. On the other hand, it did lead to some original tactics, with just a hint of St Trinian's; it happened from time to time that the ball 'got lost' under players' skirts, and young women at the very select Frances Holland School for Girls in 1897 were rebuked for keeping 'the ball too much under their petticoats'.

Even shortening the skirt was often found unacceptable; when Mary Tait, a pupil of Martina Bergman-Österberg, in 1892 began to promote the new form of sports clothing for girls that later came to be known as the gym slip, even at calf length, it was perceived by many as an affront to decency. Although the gym slip gradually gained acceptance as suitable wear for girls' gymnastic classes, it remained controversial. When as late as 1910 a Kentish member of the All-England Women's Hockey Association wore a gym slip to a match, it provoked something of a furore; and in a 1911 report of ten years' progress, Tunbridge Wells Girls' School noted that 'an annual gym display was started for [an audience of] mothers only and fathers who were doctors'. But it was not just the male gaze that was problematic. Another cause for concern was changing facilities.

Wearing the same clothes for playing muddy games like grass hockey and for returning home, often on public transport, was obviously undesirable. However, it was an option that many sportswomen chose as late as the early twentieth century, rather than face the 'indelicacy' of a communal changing room, even one for women only.

Despite this, dress reformers kept urging their case. From the 1880s onward, the Rational Dress Society protested 'against the introduction of any fashion in dress that either deforms the figure, impedes the movement of the body, or in any way tends to injure the health'. Particularly objected to were tight-fitting corsets, high-heeled and narrow-tied boots and shoes, heavily weighted skirts, crinolines and crinolinettes. Its maximum approved weight of women's clothing was seven pounds, approximately 3.2 kilogrammes, without shoes. It recommended in particular knee-length trousers, to be worn under a mid-calf skirt. In 1889 Lady Florence Harberton, a prominent member of the Rational Dress Society and a keen cyclist, was refused admission to the coffee room of a Surrey hotel while wearing rational dress of this type; she pressured the reluctant Cyclists' Touring Club into bringing an action against the hotel, which failed on a technicality.

Cycling was a particular arena for contests around femininity, and especially dress. The aforementioned Arabella Kenealy altogether disapproved of women cycling, denouncing for example in 1899 'the bicycle face … the face of muscular tension'. However, even those who generally approved of women cycling were at least in two minds on matters of dress. Sibyl Salaman, writing in *The Englishwoman* in April 1895, noted, 'That the so-called Rational Dress is becoming very general is undoubted. If a woman looks graceful in it, why not?' But already by August she was back-pedalling: 'the fact is, the dress is ugly, and never will be generally adopted by Englishwomen'; and by January 1896 she stated, 'As a practical cyclist I deny that skirts are dangerous or a hindrance to their wearers. So-called rationally-dressed women naturally feel freer without skirts, but should we not play tennis, cricket and hockey better without them?' This last point was in the nature of a rhetorical question, because as already mentioned, women hockey players were reluctant to abandon the long skirt, and although in the 1880s shops were already selling what purported to be special tennis costumes for ladies, right up to 1914, at least, women's tennis wear was basically an all-white version of contemporary summer fashions. In the course of the twentieth century women's dress gradually became more appropriate for vigorous activity, aided by the greater competitiveness accompanying the spread of the professionalisation of sport. Even so, when at the Wimbledon tennis championships as late as 1951 'Gorgeous Gussie' Moran and Maureen 'Little Mo' Connolly showed a glimpse of frilly knicker, the press professed to be scandalised. And yet there were exceptions. When it came to lacrosse, women's dress fashions were more inclined to the rational dress paradigm than women's hockey, even to the extent of insisting on dress that showed the knee; in 1901 the Ladies' Lacrosse Association encouraged players to wear tunics of 'regulation length – one inch off the ground when kneeling'.

Clubs

As sporting activities for women became more generally accepted, growing numbers of women wanted to join existing sporting clubs. The clubs themselves reacted in various ways. The Cyclists' Touring Club was formed in 1878, and from 1880 onwards it accepted women as members on equal terms with men. At the other extreme, when in 1895 the then Ladies' Hockey Association applied to affiliate to the all-male Hockey Association, it was turned down brusquely, which led to the Ladies' Hockey Association making a rule that no man could hold executive office in the LHA. Most, though by no means all, sporting clubs and associations took a similar line to that of the Hockey Association. It was generally felt that women playing alongside men would lower the standard of play, and also that men and women engaging in physical activity together was bordering on the indecent. This last view was shared by many women; and so increasingly throughout the late nineteenth and early twentieth centuries women established their own sporting clubs, independent of men.

One feature that members of women's sporting clubs had in common at least up to 1914 was that they were mainly from the affluent classes. Even if working women were able to afford the cost of subscriptions, dress and travel to and from matches, they would not have been able to attend the practices and matches, which were usually held during the day on weekdays. Still, the women who could manage these costs and inconveniences soon became very numerous, and reports of their activities were to be found in the fashionable press. Accounts follow of some of the sports in which women established their own clubs and associations, or were accepted by men's clubs.

Athletics

Athletics in general, especially as regards field and track events, has a major international profile, and the role of women in this has in the past been far from uncontested. Despite this, there has not been a great movement of athletic clubs where women's membership may have posed problems, although even here there is a degree of British exceptionalism. However, the reluctance of the IOC to accept women in athletics on the same terms as men has already been noted, and in response to this a Réunion International d'Education Physique Féminine was held at Monte Carlo in 1921 with teams representing European countries, followed later that year by an international meeting between England and France. With the success of the English teams, a Women's Association was formed in 1922 which became the Women's Amateur Athletic Association in 1926. It formulated the rules for women's athletics, organised and monitored women's athletics and offered advice on training. Universities and business houses rallied to the Association and there were soon some 23,000 members. The Association participated in the first Women's Olympic Games held in Paris in August 1922. At the first Women's International meeting held under its auspices in August 1924 at Stamford Bridge before 25,000 spectators, Great Britain won against competition from Czechoslovakia, Italy, Belgium, France and Switzerland. By the 1950s Britain was the only nation retaining separate men and women's athletic associations, and by the beginning of the twenty-first century even Britain had fallen into line. The Amateur Athletic Association now accepts both men's and women's clubs.

Cricket

This had long been played informally by well-to-do women, especially at country house Saturday-to-Mondays, and sometimes even more formally. The earliest recorded women's cricket match held in England seems to have taken place in 1745 between Bramley and Hambleton at Godsden Common, near Guildford, Surrey. Thereafter throughout the eighteenth century newspapers and magazines frequently refer to women's matches, most of them played, like their male equivalents, in Sussex, Hampshire and Surrey villages. They attracted substantial crowds and much betting, and prizes were often given, ranging from pairs of lace gloves to a barrel of ale.

The earliest formally constituted women's cricket club seems to have been the White Heather Club, based at Nun Appleton, between Tadcaster and Selby in Yorkshire, which was formed in 1887 by eight noblewomen, mainly based on the country houses of Normanhurst and Eridge, which were the seats of the noble families of Brassey and Neville. It survived as a club until 1957, and its scorebook is in the library of the Marylebone Cricket Club, the game's governing authority, at its ground at Lord's in London. In 1890 there was even a relatively short-lived professional women's cricket club called 'The Original English Lady Cricketers', which at one stage fielded two teams, and toured the country; their first match was in Liverpool. Unfortunately in 1892 its male manager disappeared, together with the club's funds. The 'Original Lady Cricketers', like the teams in some of the public matches mentioned above, may have been more remarkable for their novelty value, hence their financial advantage, than for any sporting or feminist gains.

Between then and 1914 women's cricket clubs came and went; they were mainly one-off short-lived attempts until 1926, when following a match at Colwall, Worcestershire between teams of hockey and lacrosse players seeking an alternative to tennis for a summer game, the Women's Cricket Association was formed under the leadership of Mrs Patrick Heron-Maxwell, a former president of the All-England Women's Hockey Association. The Women's Cricket Association adopted MCC laws and ran matches throughout the country. In their first season the Women's Cricket Association staged 49 games and established the popular annual cricket festival which still runs today at Colwall. By 1927 the Women's Cricket Association had 10 affiliated clubs; by 1934 this had risen to 80 and by 1938, 123 clubs had been formed. By 1931 the first county associations had emerged and a match was played between Durham and a combined Cheshire and Lancashire XI. The first public match took place in July 1929, a one day fixture between London and District and the Rest of England. In 1935 five autonomous territorial associations were set up under the umbrella of the Women's Cricket Association: East, Midlands, North, South and West. At its peak, the WCA had 208 affiliated clubs and 94 school and junior teams.

England was not the only place where women's cricket throve. It had been played in Australia since at least 1900; the Victoria Women's Cricket Association was founded in 1905 and the Australian Women's Cricket Association was founded in 1931. The English women's first international tour, to Australia, took place in 1934, when England won two tests and drew one. The England team went on to New Zealand in 1935 and won the one test that was played. The Australian women's team visited England in 1937. Three tests were played at the Oval, with even honours: one win apiece and one draw. In 1958 the International Women's Cricket Council (IWCC) was founded to organise the increasing amount of cricket, especially in Australia, New Zealand, England, South Africa, the West Indies, Denmark, and Holland.

Nowadays, however, the Women's Cricket Association is no more. On 29 March 1998 the Women's Cricket Association voted at an extraordinary general meeting to merge with the English Cricket Board, thus becoming part of a single governing body which controls cricket in England for women and men alike. The agreement itself was signed at a meeting of the Women's Cricket Association Executive Committee on 25 June 1998, and the MCC opened its doors to women a year later. In March 2004 the MCC elected its first woman committee member, Rachel Heyhoe Flint. This marks a considerable change from the days in the late 1970s when, as one of the authors recollects, Mrs Nina Popplewell, a stalwart of the Fawcett Society and a former militant suffragette, as well as being an ardent supporter of cricket, complained about only being allowed into the Pavilion at Lord's as a guest of her grandson.

Cycling

From the invention and increasingly widespread use of the safety bicycle in the 1870s, especially after the introduction of pneumatic tyres, cycling was far more than just a recreational activity, although that is how it started. It quietly revolutionised personal mobility. For those hundreds of thousands of people of both sexes and all ages from childhood on who could not afford to buy or maintain a horse, let alone a dogcart or trap, but could afford a bicycle, it meant freedom from the uncertainties of railways and omnibuses, and a degree of independence previously unimagined. It not only broke down the barriers between town and country, but to a significant extent those between the sexes. When a young lady of only moderate means went cycling it was very difficult to make sure that she was thoroughly chaperoned, and she could meet men more freely than in earlier generations. This is not to say that such female freedom was easily accepted. Cycling feminists like Ethel Smyth and Helena Swanwick in the 1890s discovered that they were often the object of jeering and catcalls, if not worse. Hence many women cyclists at this time preferred riding on specially prepared paths, or rinks, or even 'velodromes', and this was certainly friendlier

Figure 5.2 Mr and Mrs E.C. Coles Webb on their tandem, *Englishwoman*, 1896

to pneumatic tyres. This was certainly the case among society women, among whom Sibyl Salaman noted in 1895 cycling was 'all the rage this year'.

However, it is equally true that many young women were willing to brave the mockery in order to gain the extra mobility, and cycling in company helped. For this reason it was important that, as already noted, from very early on the Cyclists' Touring Club accepted women on equal terms. Local clubs also fell in line; for example, the Trafalgar Bicycle Club in 1895 boasted not only pneumatic tyres, but female membership. Also from early on there were clubs specifically for women cyclists, mainly under the aegis of the Lady Cyclists' Association, with its headquarters at 35 Victoria Street, London, SW, which was set up to provide rides, tours and other social gatherings for lady cyclists. It published a monthly journal, the *Lady Cyclists' Association News*, and a handbook (4d) which contained reliable information about country inns where ladies could be sure of being made comfortable on moderate terms. Some of the members wore rational dress. The entrance fee was one shilling and the subscription was 3s 6d annually. In 1900 the president was the Countess of Malmesbury and the honorary secretary was Miss Grace Murrell. Other early specialist publications in the 1890s included the *Lady Cyclist* and the *Wheelwoman*. Unsurprisingly, feminists took to the bicycle eagerly, and many suffragists were keen cyclists and prominent in cycling circles: for example, the militant suffragette Rose Lamartine Yates and her husband Thomas were very keen promoters of the cycling ethos in the early 1900s. In 1906 Rose was the first woman to be elected to the Council of the Cyclists' Touring Club, a triumph for women who had been unsuccessfully struggling to be represented for at least ten years.

However, as cycling became more a normal means of transport as well as a sport, professionalism tended to take over the sporting side with ever more macho extreme forms of cycling, such as the Tour de France, and again women became marginalised.

Football

Football (soccer) is one of the most controversial areas for women to intrude. Ron Atkinson, the famous England manager, expressed with typical frankness an extremely widespread attitude when he said in 1989, 'Women should be in the kitchen, the discothèque and the boutique but not in football'. This is not surprising, given that Association Football is widely regarded as the repository of the male working-class soul in most countries outside North America. Although in the late twentieth century the number of women supporters in Britain at least had grown, women playing football tends to be classed as something of an oxymoron. Many women have agreed. In reaction to a proposed women's football club in April 1895, *The Englishwoman* asseverated, 'One thing is certain, and that is that football will never and could never gain favour among Englishwomen generally'. Despite this dismissal, an underground network of women continued to play football well before 1921, when the English Football Association banned clubs affiliated to the EFA and the Football League from allowing women to use their grounds, a ban which lasted until 1971. It has been only since the 1990s that women's football has begun to achieve recognition outside its own aficionados and the freak-show media, but it has definitely made its mark. It is now the largest area of women's sports, with half a million participants in Britain alone. In 2005 the European women's championships were televised live on the BBC's main terrestrial channel. Women's football is definitely forging ahead, but it still does have some problems with certain male mentalities. In 2004 the FIFA President Sepp Blatter called for women players to wear tighter shorts, and in the course of supposedly condemning this in June 2005, the UEFA President Lennart Johansson said that sponsorship of women's football could be raised from advertising, for example by showing a 'sweaty, lovely looking girl' playing on the ground, and emerging from the changing rooms looking smart and cool. So there is some way to go yet.

Golf

This is one of the most gender-contested of games, despite the fact that in the sixteenth century two Queens, Catherine of Aragon and Mary, Queen of Scots, are recorded as playing golf, and indeed relatively few golf clubs have ever actually completely excluded women. Still, in Britain at least, it is one in which the topic of women's membership still tends to raise blood pressure, for a variety of reasons.

Golf is of course Scottish in origin, and dates back at least to the fifteenth century, although there do not seem to have been any organised clubs until the founding of the St Andrews Club, later the Royal and Ancient, in 1754 by twenty-two male members of the nobility and gentry; other clubs were soon established at Edinburgh and Musselburgh. At Musselburgh in particular the local 'Fish ladies' took to it enthusiastically, and by 1810 the Royal Musselburgh Golf Club was offering prizes to the best women golfers. In fact the social class of these women was more typical of the majority of Scottish golfers than the élite men of St Andrews; in Scotland golf always was, and remains, a popular game.

This was not the case in England, where golf remained something of an exotic importation until the mid-nineteenth century, when it quite rapidly gained considerable popularity among men of the well-to-do classes, and became one of the most popular of sports in those circles. All the same, it was in Scotland where the first tentative attempts were made to secure women's involvement in golf clubs, when in 1867 some women relatives of members of the Royal and Ancient started a small ladies' affiliate of that august institution. The St Andrews Ladies' Golf Club, as it was called, was regarded benevolently by the Royal and Ancient, and was even described as a charming feature of the Club. Of course, this was because the ladies restricted themselves to putting, and the 'charming' ladies' green was really just a putting green.

However, the main growth of women's golf clubs in the nineteenth century was based in southern England, with the formation of the Westward Ho! and North Devon Ladies' Golf Club in 1868, and the Ladies' London Scottish Club at Wimbledon in 1872, setting the pattern. Although these were women's clubs, they were usually at least affiliates of men's clubs, and most of the management as well as all the finance was in the hands of men, usually members of the corresponding men's club, as was that of the St Andrews Ladies' Club. The facilities were exiguous at best. The women were only allowed short putting greens with no hazards; they were not admitted to the main clubhouse, having to make do with a basic hut; they had to allow any men to play through, or even give way to them altogether, the slowness of women being an argument often advanced for keeping them off the main greens; and they were only allowed to use the greens at times that the men found inconvenient. The Westward Ho! Club was unusual in letting women putt fortnightly on Saturdays in the summer months; though the stipulation at this club that no member should bring a dog with her, in case it should hurt or disturb the sheep grazing nearby, leaves the impression that play was not expected to be of a serious nature. There were very few independent women's clubs, with all-women committees, and they at best had to make do with 'hen runs' of nine holes only; the cost of suitable links precluded anything more ambitious.

As time progressed, so did the position of women. Agitation in the social and political sphere had its rather more genteel counterpart in golfing circles, and gradually women's golf became less restrictive. This was given particular impetus by the formation of a Ladies' Golf Union (LGU) in 1893, in the wake of a failed attempt to organise men's clubs into a national golfing body with a nationally accepted system of handicapping. Issette Pearson, of the Wimbledon Ladies' Golf Club, with the encouragement of the scheme's devisor, Mr Laidlaw Purves, summoned a meeting of delegates of the major women's golf clubs at the Grand Hotel, Trafalgar Square, London, at which it was decided to form a national Union, with the following aims:

1   To promote the interests of the game of golf.
2   To obtain uniformity of rules.
3   To establish a uniform system of handicapping.
4   To act as a tribunal and court of reference.
5   To arrange the annual championship competition.

The Union was not to be a women-only affair. From the outset, men were made eligible to serve as executive members. Issette Pearson was the first honorary secretary, and remained in that post until 1919; the honorary treasurer was Blanch Hulton. They immediately organised a series of ladies' championships, the first taking place at Lytham St Annes, albeit on a course which Kathleen McCrone describes as 'not a severe test even for those days'. By the time of the Union's second annual general meeting, there were over 2,000 members. A *Golfer's Handbook* was compiled, giving the rules of the game, as well as a house journal called *Ladies' Golf.*

In 1911 with the growth of affiliated clubs and the need for more office space, the LGU formed a Lady Golfers' Club at 3 Whitehall Court. The Club contained a large room for meetings, luxurious furnishings and sleeping accommodation. On at least one occasion when the weather was bad, a putting competition took place on a nine hole course laid out in a large empty room. After the First World War, the dining room was described as a rest cure for those who had eaten to jazz music. In the 1960s, it merged with the Golfers' Club. By 1927 there were over 1000 clubs affiliated to the LGU, and 400 colonial clubs. Shortly after the LGU was set up, the Irish Ladies' Golf Union was formed after a meeting in Belfast. Scotland followed next in 1902 and Wales in 1904. As early as 1906 the formation of an English Ladies' Golf Association was considered, but this did not take place until 1952.

By the First World War most women's clubs were accepted adjuncts to male bodies, and women golfers were accorded a degree of respect. Even swinging and driving by women was coming reluctantly to be tolerated. In 1908 the ladies' championship was played on the Old Course at St Andrews, with the general approval of the Royal and Ancient Club, though not with all the facilities, especially for changing. Some women's clubs had eighteen hole courses, and at the 1913 Women's Open, with participants from France and the USA, as well as all over Britain, the final round was played over thirty-six holes, in the style of the men's championship. And increasingly women were being allowed to play on men's courses, though still with some ill-feeling. Signs of increasing acceptance have since included the opening in 1974 of the locker rooms and lounge of the Royal and Ancient to women on championship occasions. In 2005 women were finally permitted to compete in the Open.

According to Doreen Longrigg, in the USA, women golfers have not had to face anything like this amount of discrimination; as she writes, 'American men were proud of their lady golfers'. Still, golf in England at least had, and still has, the image of a well-to-do men's game. When suffragettes wanted to make their point to influential men, golf courses were a major target, and on several courses they carved out 'Votes for Women' on the greens; and though few women golfers were active in the women's suffrage movement, or other overtly feminist activity, their very activity has been an assertion of women's right to space. Nevertheless, the battle is far from being completely won. As indicated in Chapter 2, in most clubs women still pay a lower membership fee and green fees, have restricted access to greens and to the clubhouse. One 'horror story' cited in the House of Lords in 2002 related to a club where a white line was painted on the floor of the bar to mark the limits of women's access. Despite this, as indicated above, women golfers are not generally noted for their feminist zeal, and many are reasonably happy with the arrangements as they stand. This did not prevent the Ladies' Golf Union, still flourishing in 2002, after 109 years, from supporting a Parliamentary Bill, which was unsuccessful, aiming to apply sex discrimination law to private clubs of all sorts. Licensing law has also been used to give clubs the choice between excluding women from full membership and having a bar in the clubhouse, as in the 2002 case of the Royal West Norfolk Golf Club. This saga continues to run.

Hockey

The game of (field) hockey, played on grass, not ice, is generally reckoned to be of great antiquity, and has long been extremely popular in India and the subcontinent. In Britain, however, hockey was established relatively late. It also has had a slightly unusual image. As mentioned already, at first it was widely regarded as too rough for women, but this did not prevent it becoming very popular in girls' schools, and since it was not considered a major sport at boys' public schools, it soon became regarded somewhat ironically as a girls' game, and male grass hockey players are still regarded with a certain condescension in some circles. Originally, however, it was considered very much a male game, and the all-male Hockey Association was formed in 1886. The first private women's hockey club was founded the following year. Following the lead of the Irish Ladies' Hockey Union formed in 1892, a meeting was held in November 1895 at Westminster Town Hall of representatives of women's colleges from Oxford, Cambridge and London as private ladies' clubs. The Ladies' Hockey Association was subsequently established with Miss Lilian Faithfull, head of the Ladies' Department, King's College, London, as its president.

It has already been described how, after a rebuff from the Hockey Association for affiliation, the Ladies' Hockey Association set up the All-England Women's

Hockey Association (AEWHA). It explicitly stipulated that no man could ever hold an executive office in the Association. The first county team was formed in Sussex in 1898, to be followed by many others. Welsh and Scottish Associations were established in 1902 as was the official organ of the Association, *The Hockey Field*, issued as a weekly paper. In the same year, four territorial organisations – North , South, West and Midlands – were formed in England to administer the game. The sport became popular at school and college levels and the AEWHA was involved in making rules, fixing fees and selecting an England team. The measure of its success can be seen in the spread of the sport by the outbreak of the First World War to include five territorial and 36 county associations, more than 300 school, college and private clubs and matches at all levels including the international. By 1939, there were over 2,000 affiliated clubs. Since 1980 women's hockey has found a place in the Olympic Games, with Zimbabwe and Australia taking subsequent titles. However, in Britain it continues to have a relatively low profile, and is still associated with girls' schools; the stereotypical comedy version of an élite girls' school pupil is supposed to cry: 'Jolly Hockey Sticks'.

Lacrosse

It is remarkable that this rough Canadian game is perhaps the most stereotypical representative of the English girls' school sports, at least as much as hockey. It was first introduced into England from Canada in 1867 and by the end of the century was popular in girls' rather than in boys' schools. A Southern Ladies' Lacrosse Club was started in London in 1905; it consisted of former students of Wycombe Abbey, Roedean and Prior's Field Schools. The captain of the Club, Audrey Beaton, an old Roedeanian, subsequently established a Ladies' Lacrosse Association in 1912, mainly for schools, colleges and polytechnics. Beaton became honorary secretary and Penelope Lawrence, headmistress of Roedean, was president. In the following July, the Association issued administrative procedures and rules for international, national and county lacrosse matches. Membership of the Association was strictly limited to amateurs. By the end of the first season, there had been an increase from 20 to 70 schools and colleges as well as seven clubs. In 1913 the first international match was staged at Richmond Cricket Ground when England beat Wales and Scotland before an audience of 100 mainly women spectators. By the outbreak of the First World War the number of schools and colleges playing lacrosse rather than hockey had risen to 100 though it did not really rival the latter game in popularity.

Mountaineering

Ever since the Alpine craze struck British men in the mid-nineteenth century, and these men founded their own Alpine Club, women have been eager to join in, and after some initial reservations, have been more readily accepted than in some other sports. In the nineteenth century, women initially tended to climb in carefully guided groups, but a number of independent spirits soon launched out with only a guide, or even with just a male partner. Pictures of the time show women leaping round Alps in full Victorian fig, especially with long skirts, and this contributed to the mockery which was directed at women climbers, though not on the whole by male climbers; the French composer Edmond Audran's operetta of 1890, *Miss Helyett*, centres on a young puritanical American lady in the Pyrenees slipping and accidentally revealing quantities of frilly knicker. And yet this image can be misleading, since it seems to have become common practice for serious women Alpinists to wear climbing breeches under their skirts, and at an appropriate point far above conventional haunts to take off the skirt and give it to the guide to put it in his pack until the descent, or even leave it in a mountain hut. The latter option, however, was rather restrictive, since it meant that the return would have to be made by the same route. This seems to have led to some extra exertion by ladies who had overlooked this, and had to retrace their steps rather than face the social stigma of being seen in breeches.

Of course, climbing in the Alps, or even the Pyrenees, was too expensive for most of the young women who wanted to climb. These women took to North Wales, especially Snowdonia, and to the Lake District of England, or if a little better-off, the Scottish Highlands. This was by no means just a female interest; for many years men had been making their way up Great Gable or Cader Idris, or even Tryfan, and in 1906 the Fell and Rock Club was formed, mainly for English and Welsh weekend climbers. This club was very inclusive; members did not necessarily have to be able to lead on an ascent of Malham Cove, and indeed many of the members were less climbers than fell walkers. From the outset this had women members on the same terms as men; and the same was the case with the Midland Association of Mountaineers, started in 1908. By this time the well-to-do women were also busy organising; in 1907 the Ladies' Alpine Club was established by Mrs Aubrey 'Lizzie' LeBlond. Initially it had been the Alpine section of the Lyceum Club, but very soon set itself up as an independent entity, with rooms of its own at the Great Central Hotel in London, by Marylebone Station. It prided itself on being the only Alpine club exclusively for women. At first the men's Alpine Club was dubious about this development, but soon became supportive; the fact that the Ladies' Alpine Club's Honorary President was Queen Margherita of Italy may have influenced their change of attitude. The Ladies' Alpine Club was much more than just a centre to co-ordinate women's climbing activity; it had many of the features of a social club in the generally understood sense of the word. It provided members with tea, bread and butter and cake in front of a coal fire for a mere nine pence, and organised monthly lectures and At Homes. They published a *Ladies' Alpine Club Journal*, and from 1913 their own Year Book. During the First World War, their rooms were commandeered by the War Department, but restored in 1919. They soon made international contacts, particularly through Lyceum Club connections, and the war had its effect on these, which was far from negative. For example, Swiss women had traditionally thought of climbing as an activity centred on crazy English tourists, but the drastic disappearance of tourists, especially British, during the war, led to the formation of the Schweizerische

Frauen Alpen Club in 1918, with strong links with the Ladies' Alpine Club; and later still, it had close relations with the Royal Netherlands Alpine Club, formed in 1936 to recognise the deep yearning of Dutch women, especially those from Holland proper, for land higher than 50 metres. At the time of writing, the Ladies' Alpine Club continues to flourish, although its name has become somewhat misleading; its members are more likely to be confronting especially vertiginous pitches in the Andes, or the Himalayas.

Another effect of the First World War was to deprive British lady Alpinists of their preferred haunts, and so they sought recreation nearer home, particularly in North Wales, where many of the climbs made up in challenge what they lacked in altitude. Indeed, there were women who came to prefer these climbs, and it was to bring together such women that a letter was published in the *Manchester Guardian* in 1920 inviting women who were interested to form their own society. On 21 March 1921, a meeting was held at the Pen-y-Gwryd Hotel at the foot of Snowdon in North Wales. The chair was taken by Mrs Eleanor 'Len' Winthrop Young, with her husband Geoffrey, who had lost a leg above the knee in the War (though this apparently only slightly limited his climbing), both of whom were prominent members of the Fell and Rock Club. At this meeting an organisation was formed whose initial title was the Women's Rock Climbing Club, soon changed to the Pinnacle Club. It had its own hut at Cwm Dyli in Nant Gwynant, and its president for many years was Emily 'Pat' Kelly. Despite the fact that the founding meeting took place at Pen-y-Gwryd, which gives its name to the far from challenging 'PyG track' up Snowdon, qualifications for membership were moderately demanding, involving the ability to lead on an 'ordinary difficult climb'. What constituted an 'ordinary difficult climb' grew more exacting over the years. In the 1960s a (male) climber of an older generation was slightly taken aback to read in an account of a climb: 'At this point the pitch eased off to the vertical'. Women by then were at least as likely as men to tackle angles of 270 degrees. The Pinnacle Club in particular aimed to develop a more professional attitude to difficult rock climbing and mountaineering, and develop confidence and good leadership for local expeditions. By the time of its 60th anniversary in 1981, the society consisted of 150 members, and parties had tackled mountains ranging from the Himalayas to those in New Zealand. The Pinnacle Club still continues, like the Ladies' Alpine Club, to demonstrate that women can hold their own with men on mountains.

Tennis

Male–female relationships in tennis have in the past been almost as fraught as those in golf, which is surprising, for a number of reasons. Lawn tennis, as distinct from 'Real' (or 'Royal') Tennis, was a development of the social game of rackets, and only became organised in the later nineteenth century. Previously, it had been regarded, like croquet, very much as a country house and garden party game, with both sexes playing decorously, and initially Wimbledon was the centre of the All-England Croquet Club which admitted women on equal terms with men. Again, in a game like croquet, as in hockey, long skirts gave opportunities for somewhat dubious tactics. However, croquet was of limited interest, as compared to the faster-moving and more exciting game of tennis, and so in 1877 the club altered its name to the All-England Croquet and Lawn Tennis Club; and soon it changed the word order to The All-England Lawn Tennis and Croquet Club. For reasons which are far from clear, this spelt a drastic change in the club's attitude to women; apparently, documentation that might explain this has not survived, since the earliest minutes available date from 1883. The club immediately organised a men's singles championship but refused to accommodate women at this level. Women tennis players were better suited by tournaments held by clubs at Dublin (1879), Bath (1881), the Northern Association (1882) and Cheltenham (1883). By this time Wimbledon was compelled reluctantly to admit women to membership, given that they paid the same fee as men, but with severe restrictions: they were prohibited from holding any positions of authority, and denied access to the ground after 2 o'clock on Saturday afternoons, when the men wanted it. In 1884 Wimbledon somewhat belatedly did set up an annual Ladies' Championship, though at first only of three sets, and with a cash prize rather than a cup. The first championship was won by Maud Watson, whose victory was due among other things to her employment of the then relatively novel (for women at least) over-arm service. In 1886 the All-England Club finally relented to the extent of presenting the winner of the Ladies' Championship with a challenge cup, the ultimate sign of acceptability in the world of sport. Despite the received impression that women were less able to cope with prolonged activity than men, women did not have the male relief of a bye into the final round, which the men had until 1886; and in 1885 Maud Watson not only successfully defended her title, but played in more open competitions than the male champion.

Wimbledon's relationship to women is interesting in that it long seemed to have a traditionally masculine, not to say macho, attitude to the sport. While clubs throughout Britain and Ireland were happily admitting women to full membership, the All-England Club long continued to be reluctant to accommodate them. This was especially noticeable in the matter of doubles. By 1886 Wimbledon had admitted a full women's singles championship, in parallel with the men's singles and men's doubles, but it continued to resist the very idea of women's doubles, which they claimed would bring an element of 'pat-ball' to an otherwise serious event. From 1899 to 1907 with extreme reluctance the club did grudgingly allow non-championship women's doubles, but then banned them again until, after considerable pressure from the Lawn Tennis Association, they finally instituted a Ladies' Doubles championship in 1913. Mixed doubles, however, were another matter altogether, which is especially surprising. These after all had long been the most popular part not only of the informal country-house game, but of tennis clubs throughout Britain, adding to their reputation, at least as late as the 1950s, as an approved venue for middle-class courting second only to the local Conservative Association. However, the All-England Club was concerned not with social interaction but with serious play, and this was felt to be impossible with mixed doubles. It was assumed that the male players would be much stronger than their female partners, and would therefore have ungallantly to monopolise the game, or else hold themselves back out of chivalrous motives to allow the little woman the chance to hit the occasional ball. At best, the woman was always assumed to have a secondary role in mixed doubles, which were in any case considered to be rather frivolous affairs. This frame of mind persisted well into the twentieth century. Although the Northern Association had introduced mixed doubles championships in 1888, and these had become popular throughout Britain and Ireland, Wimbledon held out against them until in 1913 the Lawn Tennis Association compelled them to comply. Yet even now the attitude of at least some male players seems close to that of the Australian John Newcombe, who pronounced that at Wimbledon 'the ladies are simply the cherries on the cake'.

As noted, Wimbledon was unusual in its attitude to women in tennis. This has long been recognised as a sport in which women can, and do, excel, which is one of the reasons why boys' public schools have in the past been extremely reluctant to provide facilities for it. However, as tennis has become increasingly professionalised, the pressure of money has caused even Wimbledon to fall into line. And to complete the irony, although the All-England Club insists that its colours are purple and green, they traditionally have white added, so that fans alighting at Southfields Station find themselves faced by the colours of the Women's Social and Political Union, members of which in 1913 only just failed to burn down the club's stands, then in central Wimbledon.

Other sports

This category does not reflect the importance of sports other than those mentioned above, but their relevance to our theme. For example, swimming is extremely popular both for men and women, but most non-professional swimmers are not interested in clubs, although there are and have been such clubs. For example, in 1892 a Ladies' Tadpole Swimming Club was formed at Kensington Baths, whose members swam in a uniform costume of navy blue twill, with a scarlet sailor collar and trimmings. This was obviously a means for women to learn how to swim in the days before mixed bathing was generally accepted; the National Vigilance Association was still opposing it as late as 1930. Again, although women had taken part in the national championships of the Amateur Swimming Association since 1901, water polo had its problems, since men as usual tended to take priority in local swimming baths, which again led to a certain separatist movement. In 1923 the Southern Counties Ladies' Water-Polo Association was formed in order to assert the right of women to play at water polo. It was rapidly followed by a number of other regional groups.

Sculling for women was already accepted before 1900, but it was only in 1926 that the Women's Amateur Rowing Association was founded, and in the following year the Ladies' Boat Race between Oxford and Cambridge was held on the Isis over half a mile. The Association's objects were to maintain among women the standard of oarsmanship as recognised by amateur rowing clubs, to hold a regatta or regattas if and when so determined by the committee, such regattas to be mainly or exclusively for women, and to promote the interests of boat racing generally among women. The Association suspended its activities during the Second World War, but returned with vigour thereafter. The first European championships were held in 1954. Both the Amateur Rowing Association and the Women's Amateur Rowing Association had affiliated to the International Rowing Federation in 1947, and in 1961 the latter was incorporated into the Amateur Rowing Association, ending at last the very idea of discrimination.

Traditional field sports are also an area where women, particularly of the upper classes, have always participated, although following a hunt while riding side-saddle must have created problems when a large fence or other obstacle presented itself. Shooting was also popular, but not just of the shotgun variety. A Ladies' Rifle Club flourished at the beginning of the twentieth century with its headquarters at Brighton. Bisley rules and regulation targets were used. The entry fee in 1912 was 10 shillings. Clubs sprang up around the country and in 1910 the National Rifle Association admitted the first Ladies' Club to affiliate. A Ladies' Bisley was subsequently held with members using the service rifle and competing on equal terms with men.

Of course, not all sports and other recreational activities are as energetic as the above. Mention has already been made of women's snooker. The slightly more aristocratic sport of billiards, as played by Mozart among others, has also had its female devotees. In Britain, the Women's Billiards Association was founded in 1931 with the objects of encouraging, promoting and controlling women's billiards, and sponsoring championships and other competitions, team matches and tournaments. Its president was the Viscountess Elibank, the chairman, Mrs Longman and vice-chairman, Teresa Billington-Greig, whose husband just happened to be a billiard table salesman. Most of the council members were also members of the Lyceum Club. Its headquarters were at 17 Buckingham Palace Gardens, London SW1, by courtesy of the Women's Automobile and Sports Association. It is uncertain when this Association expired, but as mentioned in Chapter 2, the Ladies' Snooker Association has been keeping up the pressure.

In field sports and even in table sports, it can be argued that discrimination is justified by women's comparative lack of physical strength, or even hand-eye co-ordination. However, this cannot be said to apply to such activities as chess or bridge, which still have had, and continue to have, their discriminatory problems. Although there were women's chess clubs in the Netherlands as early as 1847, organised women's chess does not seem to have started in Britain until the 1880s, when the Brighton Chess Club had a ladies' branch which ran tournaments, and it was only in 1895 that the Ladies' Chess Club was established in London. For a long time women were segregated in clubs, partly on the grounds that they played less well than the men. Reasons adduced by the women have been their relative lack of time and resources, and that they

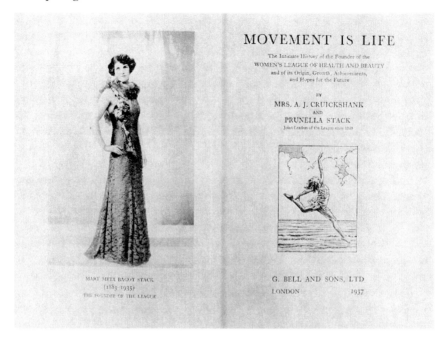

Figure 5.3 History of the Women's League of Health and Beauty, and the League's logo, 1935

were more subject to interruption. Similarly, in *Why Women Lose at Bridge*, Joyce Nicholson quotes Jakob Armanson of Iceland: 'Women do not have equal rights to leisure time'. She goes on to adduce the following reasons for women's relatively poor performance. First, women in general have less free time and available money than men. Time is especially important; it takes time to study the game, to play as much as possible and to sit in on games and 'kibitz' leading players to study their tactics. Next, women's upbringing and general social conditioning tends to be oriented towards co-operation, and away from aggression and competition – the 'will to win'. Finally, and extremely importantly, women are often undermined by men's attitudes. When faced with an assumption that they will fail, it is even more difficult for women to summon up the confidence to succeed.

Overall, it is apparent that women organising for sport has traditionally been something that male-oriented sports organisations have long resisted, but that over time, this resistance has been worn down. Even so, women's sport and men's sport still exist in separate categories. Would a merger of the two into completely mixed sports finally prove that men's superior athletic ability would leave women behind in all categories? Or might it prove something different? So far that has never been tried, and in any case such a result would be outside the remit of this study unless it was part of the activity of an actual sporting club.

Health, beauty ... and fitness

In the late nineteenth and early twentieth centuries physical exercise and 'fitness' came to be regarded as increasingly important. As outlined above, in opposition to the traditional condemnation of any vigorous exercise for women, an equally strong mainly eugenist movement had grown in the nineteenth century, intended mainly to improve women's childbearing capabilities in order to produce a 'fit' population. The concept of 'the fit', and even more, 'the unfit', was strongly influenced by ideas usually attributed nowadays to an ideology of Social Darwinism, in which 'the unfit' were deemed an evolutionary error, and should not be allowed to reproduce their kind, or even to exist at all. Although very few movements promoting healthy exercise had an explicitly eugenic agenda, many did find themselves expressing aims not far removed from that. An ideal in many quarters was that of the supposed ancient Greek concept of 'the good and beautiful', and especially where women were concerned an effort was made to combine physical effort with grace and beauty, whence the popularity of 'Greek dancing' as promoted by Isidora Duncan among others. Thus the growth of the 'keep fit' movement throughout the last quarter of the twentieth century, with consequent amounts of money being made from expensive gyms and 'no pain, no gain' programmes, was far from being the novelty it was sometimes claimed to be; the term 'keep fit' in this sense seems to have been first used in 1929.

The main body that promoted physical exercise for women by combining it with these aesthetic ideals in fact drew its initial inspiration not from ancient Greece, but modern India. This was the Women's League of Health and Beauty, an independent self-supporting commercial enterprise, established by Mary 'Molly' Bagot Stack in 1930, and continued by her daughter Prunella Stack. As the wife of an officer in a Gurkha regiment, Mrs Stack was inspired by the graceful movement of Indian women, and followed this up by studying basic yoga techniques with a Mr Gopal. On returning to Britain, she set about promoting her own system of exercises, and eventually established the League. Originally called the Build-the-Body-Beautiful League, it was designed 'for business girls and busy women to enable them to conserve and improve their physique'. It did not entirely escape eugenic associations. Its original stated aim was 'Racial Health', which gave a misleading impression of the League: it referred to the betterment of the human race, and not any single part of it. However, even when modified in 1936 to 'Racial Health Leading to Peace', the impression was not exactly helped when at a Berlin meeting in 1938 the League's contingent actually gave the raised-arm Nazi salute, which the young Prunella Stack at the time naïvely regarded as a mere gesture of politeness towards the hosts of the event. This is unfortunate, because in practice the League has been multi-racial, and has not discriminated by income. Originally, at a time when an average office worker's weekly pay was three guineas, the annual subscription was 2/6d, with an entry fee of 2/-, and 6d for each class; costs that were far from prohibitive. The League enjoyed immediate popularity, which inspired a host of commercial competitors. Unlike these, however, and more in keeping with its contemporary organisations in nationalist and Marxist regimes, to say nothing of Busby Berkeley films, it also arranged mass gymnastic displays, which were originally inspired by the Czech 'Sokol' movement. It was particularly noted for its 'uniform' of white blouse and black knickers. Its organs were *Beauty* and later *Mother and Daughter.* Its real heyday in this form was the 1930s, but it has continued to operate, modifying its public aspect and its organisation in response to changing circumstances without, however, substantially changing its aims. In the twenty-first century its successor organisation continues under the title of The Fitness League (TFL), which is sponsored by Sport England and Sport Scotland. It teaches rhythmic exercise to music. The TFL Technique is based on encouraging correct posture which releases the body's potential for good health. It claimed in 2004 over 14,000 members, and runs classes in Canada, Ireland, Netherlands, South Africa, Zimbabwe, New Zealand and Pakistan. Further details can be found on its website. Fortunately, the association of 'fitness' with eugenics had vanished long before the millennium. The days of mass gymnastic displays, however, are also long gone. 'Fitness' nowadays tends to mean solitary concentration on one's own body, with nobody else involved except possibly one's personal trainer.

Major sources for this chapter

These are varied, as is the nature of individual sports; those wanting further information on specific sports should check the Bibliography. More generally, for the period up to 1914 in Britain, all but the most serious researchers should be more than satisfied with Kathleen McCrone's exhaustive and yet highly readable *Sport and the Physical Emancipation of Women 1870–1914. Sporting Females* by Jennifer Hargreaves, and *Women in Sport*, edited by Gerda L. Cohen, are also useful for more recent developments. To put women and sport into context, we refer you to Neil Tranter's *Sport, Economy and Society in Britain 1750–1914.* Periodicals have also been useful; among those aimed at the general reader, the *Englishwoman* is particularly interesting for the 1890s. More recently the daily press (especially *The Times, Daily Telegraph, Guardian* and *Independent*) has been a valuable source of updated information.

6 Clubs for girls

Early years

Girls' clubs were from their beginning very different from women's clubs, and this is by no means merely a question of the age of the membership. As organised from the 1880s until the First World War, they were not altogether the sort of bodies that girls from well-to-do families would want to join, despite the protestations of their organisers. They were above all for teenage girls who had to go out to work to contribute to the family income, in mills, or factories, or shops, or on pit brows. Unlike the vast majority of women's clubs, girls' clubs were not organised on the members' own initiative – indeed, the girls' participation was initially at least expected to be largely passive: they were there less to do good than to have good done to them. The impetus for starting girls' clubs was definitely philanthropic; there was a belief among nineteenth-century philanthropists, apparently shared by some twentieth-century historians, that working class culture was monolithic, and consisted largely of effing and blinding, drunkenness and incest. It was therefore necessary to rescue the girls from this, both for their own sakes, and as an attempt to 'elevate' the working class as a whole. A later commentator described the programme of the pioneers of girls' clubs as a 'social ambulance' and many clubs appear to have been run at least initially in order to provide an alternative to the streets, in one sense or another. Indeed, this was part of a general concern about the state of society, and especially of the 'lower depths', the denizens of which were perceived in some quarters to be barely human, and that this had major evolutionary implications; H.G. Wells' effete Eloi and predatory subterranean Morlocks in his 1895 story *The Time Machine* are a later expression of this anxiety. In the interests of society as a whole it was felt that something should be done about this. Among other things, by 1880 various bodies had been organising boys' clubs for some years with the minimum aim of 'rescuing' at least a saving remnant from base culture, but preferably raising the working class as a whole by instilling the masculine virtues of a sort of muscular Christianity (most of these clubs had a markedly religious basis). Organisations concerned with the welfare of girls were set up, most prominently the Young Women's Christian Association and the Girls' Friendly Society.

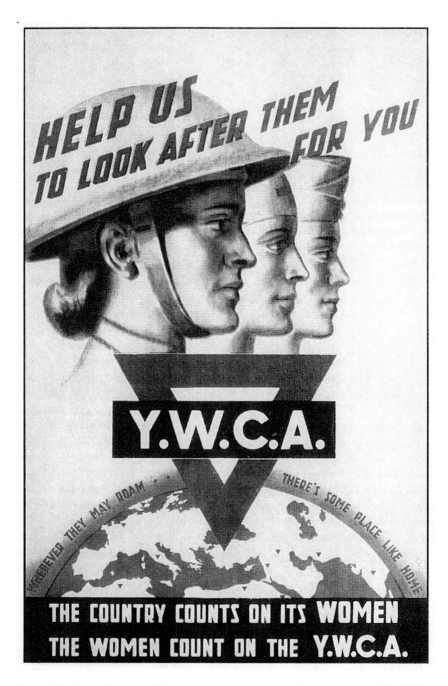

Figure 6.1 Young Women's Christian Association poster from the Second World War. 91 leave hostels had been provided by 1944

Young Women's Christian Association

The Young Women's Christian Association (YWCA) was the brainchild of two women who were initially unknown to each other, Mary Jane Kinnaird and Emma Robarts. As early as 1855, Miss Robarts, living in then rural Barnet, Middlesex, formed a group of 23 young women to 'offer their service with their prayers'. Realising the vast possibilities for spreading the Christian message, Robarts was responsible for an organisation called the Prayer Union which by 1859 had branches in all parts of the United Kingdom. In one of her early leaflets, Robarts asked, 'Is it not well from time to time to take a clear and steady view of the simple, world-wide object of a Young Women's Christian Association, the spiritual benefit, the eternal salvation of the young of our own sex?' From the outset, she stated that 'the several divisions of class, ranging from princesses, the daughters of the middle classes, young wives and mothers, shop women, domestic servants and factory girls, should be encouraged to join'.

In the same year that Robarts formed her first prayer group, Mary Kinnaird, the mother of seven children and daughter of a Scottish Liberal MP, began to work towards the same end. Living in central London, she gathered seamstresses and milk girls for an after dinner Bible class, claimed by her daughter to be the first women's club in England. This was at a time when the Crimean War gave rise to a need for accommodation for nurses going to and returning from Russia. Kinnaird therefore opened a YWCA hostel at 51 Upper Charlotte Street, London, and a few years later launched an appeal to extend the London house for 'that large class of young women employed in business, destitute of friends'. Another hostel was opened in Bristol in 1862.

An interesting feature of Kinnaird's activities was the establishment of three Evening Homes in London, which were equipped with classrooms and libraries. After consuming a free tea, the girls attended the Bible class twice a week, and they were also encouraged to improve their reading and writing skills. Rural areas were also catered for. District Referees toured their own counties, meeting groups of girls, often up to 100 in number in villages, where weekly classes were held. A typical monthly programme would consist of a Bible class, a social gathering, a sewing meeting, and general educational classes; and once a quarter, a speaker from the YWCA might address them on such subjects as thrift, reading, foreign missions and duties of membership.

It was a logical step for the two organisations sharing the same title and with overlapping functions to amalgamate: Robarts' Association did not attempt to found homes or raise funds and Kinnaird's Association had its strongest base in London. The new YWCA was founded in 1877 with Lord Shaftesbury as its President. Its first badge, with the motto 'By love serve one another', was drawn up by the Total Abstinence Department. With its greater resources, the Association gathered momentum, making its greatest impact in the larger cities. By 1897, there were 25 hostels in London, 100 in the rest of England and Wales, 10 in Scotland and 14 in Ireland.

The success of the movement in the last quarter of the nineteenth century can be attributed to a number of causes. On the religious aspect, the evangelical tours of Great Britain by the two Americans, Dwight L. Moody and Ira D. Sankey, in the 1870s and 1880s proved to be a great stimulus to the movement. Many girl members played in the bands which accompanied the speakers at their meetings and attended revivalist sessions. The leading women of the Association also entertained Moody and Sankey in their London homes. Prayer meetings benefited by an increase in numbers and the mission's handbook *Songs and Solos* stimulated a new interest in the Association's choirs.

Events in the social and moral climate of the time also affected the work of the YWCA. There had for some time been much concern about what came to be called 'White Slavery', the presumed abduction of young women and girls for prostitution, and this was given wide publicity by the revelations of child prostitution in London by W.T. Stead in the *Pall Mall Gazette* in July 1885 under the heading 'The Maiden Tribute of Modern Babylon' – revelations which helped speed the passing of the 1885 Criminal Law Amendment Act, which (among other things) raised the age of consent from 13 to 16. The Association immediately began to mount patrols in parks and at railway stations and raised funds for 'Prevention and Protection' work. In the same year, the Travellers' Aid Society, consisting of 17 organisations concerned with this work, such as the Girls' Friendly Society and the Metropolitan Association for Befriending Young Servants, was formed: it was at the Association's Old Cavendish Street offices that the Executive Committee held its first meeting.

An innovative social experiment was carried out by the committee of the house at 55 Welbeck Street when it decided to open a dining room for business girls, after observing that many of them were walking up and down the streets during their dinner hour. In a short time, the dining room proved to be too small to meet the demand. This led to the purchase of the Welbeck House and Restaurant at 101 Mortimer Street in 1884, providing hot meals at low prices. Seating only 60 diners, this too soon proved to be inadequate. Two years later, the branch moved to 116 Regent Street and housed a restaurant which overflowed into the gymnasium and catered for 100 people. Near to it was a well-stocked reading room which was open from 10 a.m. to 10 p.m.

The Association was run on reasonably democratic lines. Unlike the Girls' Friendly Society, which required every Associate to be a member of the Established Church and of assured moral standing, the Association embraced other denominations and understood the temptations of city life. No age limit was imposed on membership, which was renewed on an annual basis. A special Junior Department was set up in 1884 for work amongst children and in 1912 the first YWCA Girl Guides company was formed. The Association was also the initiator of movements which subsequently split off in order to cater for specialist interests. A good example is the Nurses' Union, formed in 1886 and which had a thriving membership; in 1917, with new developments, it became the College of Nursing. Similarly, the Factory Helpers' Union, also formed in 1886, became the Federation of Working Girls' Clubs.

Missionary work was one of the Association's earliest concerns. Many of the women in the movement were either daughters or wives of missionaries. The first colonial branch was established at Port Dover, Ontario in the 1870s. Other branches were formed in India (1875), New Zealand (1877), Singapore (1877), Australia (1879) and later, Japan, the United States of America and Africa. In 1894 the World YWCA was founded with its offices initially in London, followed three years later by the first World Conference, also held in London, with 300 representatives from 20 countries. Topics for discussion included women's duties towards the State, the intellectual and moral training for women, and Christianity and womanhood. Subsequently the Conference was held in different parts of the world.

A variety of literature helped to keep members well informed. The first was *Our Own Gazette*, followed in 1881 by the *Monthly Letter* and *Young Ladies*. By 1897, the *Gazette* claimed to have the second largest paid circulation of any women's publication. Name changes were not uncommon as well as a number of new publications. There was *The Home Friend*, *Go Forward*, *Our Own Gazette*, and the *Quarterly Journal*, later *New Outlook*, and *Update*. A novel way of publicising the Association's work from 1876 was the issuing of cards which could be 'carried in the Bible, purse or hand, [so that] fellow members of the YWCA may recognise one another in railway carriage, meeting, or elsewhere'.

Girls' Friendly Society

The origins of the Girls' Friendly Society (GFS) can be traced back to the appearance of the report in 1873 of Mrs Jane Nassau Senior, the first woman Inspector for Workhouses and District Schools, on the distressed conditions of many 'children of the State'. Within a year, in May 1874, a meeting was held in Lambeth Palace consisting of a clergyman, Mrs Nassau Senior, Mrs Archibald Tait, wife of the Archbishop of Canterbury, Mrs Harold Brown, wife of the Bishop of Winchester, and Mrs Mary Townsend, wife of a Conservative MP, who became the driving force of the Girls' Friendly Society. In January 1875 the Society was formed with its aim 'to band together in one society women and girls as Associates and Members for mutual help (religious and secular) for sympathy and prayer' and its motto 'Bear ye one another's burdens'. It was to become extensively run by women for women. Unlike other societies for 'fallen women' it was intended to prevent illegitimacy which was often the result of friendlessness and loneliness. The organisation was on a diocesan basis under the patronage of the bishop. Associates, who had to be members of the Church of England, chose members to represent them on the Diocesan Council, which in turn sent delegates to the Central Council. The initiative was widely welcomed and within six years of its founding, the Society had 47,000 members.

Associates were ladies of good standing, at first often from aristocratic backgrounds, who saw their task as inculcating religious values in their charges, and more generally improving their education and behaviour. Responsibility for individual girls was taken seriously, and the presentation of small gifts to them was encouraged. Members, who did not have to be communicants of the Church of England, could be enrolled as early as eight years of age. The Central

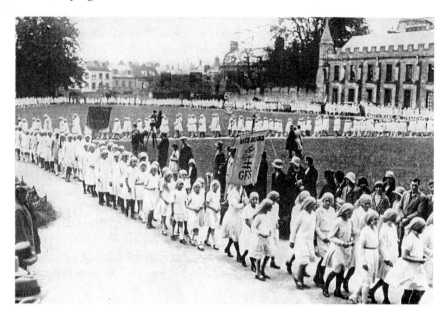

Figure 6.2 Procession of Girls' Friendly Society candidates, Wells Cathedral Green, June 1931

Rules of the Society included the stipulation, 'No girl who has not borne a virtuous character to become admitted as a Member; such character being lost, the Member to forfeit her Card'. When one Associate, Mrs Papillon, claimed that urban girls' virginity should not be taken for granted, the Bishops combined with the Chairman of the Society to defeat Papillon's motion. As a result she resigned and founded the Young Women's Help Society. It was not until 1936 that a girl who had had an illegitimate child could remain a Member. Married women were also excluded from being Members. Prayers and Bible study were important parts of the Society's activities, though there were incentives such as country holidays, fêtes, prizes for thrift, reading courses, sewing classes, and GFS books containing suitable literature.

As domestic service was one of the largest forms of employment in the nineteenth century, it is not surprising that servants often formed a majority of the Members, though the Society aimed without great success to attract young women in urban centres. The image of the GFS as essentially aimed at working class girls and women deterred many who were in clerical or professional occupations: these tended to be attracted by the work of the Young Women's Christian Association. The dangers of the city were emphasised by the Society, and approved lodging houses provided under supervision wherever possible.

Although as has been made clear the GFS was essentially organised by middle or upper class élite, it was not seen only as a source for recruiting servants. Brian Harrison has shown that the Society made efforts to improve the status of domestics. By 1883, 48 Registry Offices had been opened and in 1905 a Central

Employment Office had been established. Special booths were opened at fairs opposed to the recruitment of servants through the hiring fair, and in the first decade of the twentieth century the society collaborated with the Mothers Union for state registration of servants' registries.

One means of spreading news and views between branches was the official publications, *Friendly Leaves*, later the *Girls' Society Quarterly*, the *Girls' Friendly Society Advertiser*, later the *Associates Journal and Advertiser*, *Friendly Work* and the *Girls' Friendly Society Associate Journal* and other literature. Examples of the latter could be addressed either to Associates or Members. Some contained constructive suggestions, such as one pamphlet by Lady Louisa Knightley, President of the Peterborough Diocesan Council, entitled *Hints on the Work of the Girls' Friendly Society in Country Parishes* (1883) and Mrs Townsend's *A Friendly Letter to Fathers and Mothers about the Girls' Friendly Society* (1884).

Although the Society was an all-female organisation, there was little evidence that it promoted policies which espoused women's causes. The women's suffrage movement, for example, was considered to be subversive and the Society took no part in the campaign to promote women's property rights, workers' rights or the reform of the divorce laws. Participation in politics was, at first, avoided: the assumption of Tory anti-Republican values was made manifest in the Society's literature and activities of the Associations. However, the GFS proved a ready source of recruitment for the Primrose League, formed in 1883 'for the maintenance of religion and of the Constitution of the Realm and of the Imperial Ascendancy of Great Britain'. It encouraged the involvement of friends into small groups called habitations, which promoted Conservative principles and became active canvassing bodies during election campaigns. Women played a prominent part at such times and willing recruits were drawn from the ranks of GFS Associates.

The Society did not confine its activities to the United Kingdom. Considering the number of women who had taken posts abroad as governesses, nurses and maids, the GFS recognised that part of its work needed to be extended. In 1882, Lady Mary Woolf was appointed the first Correspondent (later President) of the English Communities Abroad. Within six years the society had Associates in such places as Gibraltar, Lisbon, Naples, Constantinople, Odessa and Smyrna.

On a much larger scale was the Society's work in the field of emigration. The leading figure in this initiative was the Hon. Mrs Ellen Joyce, who stated, 'It is the most practical bit of religious work that anyone can take up. Its missionary influence is the largest: it is missionary work done by hundreds instead of by units!' The supervision of girls and women from departure to arrival and installation in new homes was in the hands of the GFS. It was as late as 1920 that these travelling arrangements were handed over to another body, the Society for the Overseas Settlement of British Women. Settlement was in many different parts of the Empire, ranging from New Zealand to British Columbia and arranged with the co-operation of the Agent-General for each colony. These were followed by visits from Mrs Joyce and others. In Canada, for instance, on her second visit there Mrs Joyce attended a conference held in Montreal of

Associates from all branches. The link between religion and imperialism was thus strengthened by the work of the Society.

In the United Kingdom, from the Society's early days, locally organised meetings of members in clubs were widespread. This took place in recreation rooms, many of which were not purpose built. It was not until after the First World War that the GFS Club came into its own. The range of activities was governed by three objectives, friendship, recreation and reconstruction. Though the activities varied from branch to branch, they included classes in citizenship, recitation, singing and dancing, and the mounting of missionary and mystery plays. In 1924 there were over 350 registered clubs, under the supervision of a Club Organiser. In the same year the London headquarters, Townsend House, purchased by members' own subscriptions, was opened. It also provided accommodation for women. A different strand from 1914 was the development of the Guide movement within the confines of the GFS. There were also special 'Weeks' under a variety of titles, such as Study Weeks and Holiday Weeks, providing many different experiences, including picnics, fancy dress suppers, talks, theatricals, visits to famous buildings and beauty spots, all with the aim of recruiting GFS Members.

An unusual social experiment was undertaken by the Society in 1921. The *White Horse* in Woolwich, South London, a famous public house, had been purchased in order to convert it into a social centre, with accommodation for unmarried mothers, and a refuge. By 1924 it had provided 2,000 nights lodgings for girls and women. The club offered a wide range of recreational activities in the evenings, and was remarkable for being open to boys as well as girls. The *White Horse* scheme, serving the local community, was emulated in other parts of England.

By this time GFS membership was changing. The monopoly of the Church of England in attracting young women to their activities was being challenged by other denominations and from the 1890s recruitment of suitable Associates had become a problem. More importantly many Members who had entered into domestic service in the Society's early days were now employed in shops and factories, and were less likely to seek membership. The ideal of imperialism in its missionary aspect had also begun to fade. However, although the First World War proved to be a watershed in the Society's history, even in 1933 there were over 150,000 Members organised in 2,256 branches.

'Clubs for working girls'

It was working with a boys' club that led one particular woman not only to establishing a girls' club independent of such organisations as the YWCA and the GFS, but eventually writing what came to be regarded as the authoritative work on clubs for girls, entitled *Clubs for Working Girls*. She was the Hon. Maude Stanley.

By the 1870s it was becoming usual for upper-class ladies to become involved in social work in slum areas, particularly in London. In fact, in the late nineteenth century it seemed almost fashionable for young women of the upper classes to gain some experience in running girls' clubs; Margot Tennant, the society beauty who later married Liberal Prime Minister Herbert Asquith and eventually became Lady Oxford, was just one such well-to-do young woman. But by no means all of these upper-class women were just briefly descending, or condescending, on the poor in order to gain fashionable experience of social work. Many of them were highly motivated, and devoted much of their lives to mitigating the effects of urban poverty; prominent among these was Maude Stanley. She came from an aristocratic background: she was the third daughter of Baron Stanley of Alderley, and her sister Rosalind became the Countess of Cumberland. However, she also had strong links with reformers, such as William Morris, Octavia Hill and Henry Solly. In addition to her work with boys' and girls' clubs, she was also at various times a Poor Law Guardian, a Manager of the Metropolitan Asylums Board and a Governor of the Borough Polytechnic. Initially, as already noted, she had been concerned not with girls, but with boys, in the poor and squalid Five Dials area of London (around what is now Charing Cross Road and Shaftesbury Avenue, abutting on Soho), where ironically she was the ground landlord of many of the premises she so deplored. She had become concerned about the moral and intellectual welfare of the boys who hung around the streets, 'who from their very civility to myself, I felt were open to the refining influence of a woman's teaching'. In 1873 she set up a Sunday School for some of the more promising of these boys, with the help of a few local men, whose patience and temper were severely tested by the work: 'as for mine, I felt it no trial, for the fact of contending with the determined mischief of some of the boys, had in it the delight of a fight, in which I was generally victorious'. She then turned her attention to the girls, establishing the Soho Club for Girls in 1880, which soon had premises at 59 Greek Street.

Setting up a girls' club in the later nineteenth century called for different emphases to boys' clubs; muscular Christianity was hardly appropriate. The specific concern for girls was not at first because of any pro-feminist sentiment, but rather emanated from the 'separate spheres' ideology of the time, according to which women were indeed, if uncorrupted, a 'refining influence'; therefore improving a girl's moral outlook would make her capable of elevating her menfolk and her class as a whole. There was also the implication that this would prepare them for a conventional role in marriage and motherhood. In fact, these soon became secondary considerations, as Maude Stanley seems increasingly to have felt that it was worth trying to 'elevate' the girls for their own sake. Her Soho Club was open every evening, and had a strict programme: girls attended classes in drawing, French, singing, needlework, music, gymnastics and mathematics. There was a library, a tea-room, a medical dispensary and even cheap residential accommodation for 'Young Women engaged in business, and students'. In fact, membership of the club was not that cheap: one shilling entrance fee, and two shillings a quarter thereafter. This was obviously not for the lowest of the low, but for 'respectable' girls.

As already indicated, Maude Stanley was not alone. Extensive networks of clubs were already being established by the Young Women's Christian Association and the Girls' Friendly Society, but also by the Church Army and various settlements, notably the Women's University Settlement, the Lady Margaret Hall Settlement, the Canning Town Settlement (with its 'Time and Talents' organisation), and the Wesleyan Bermondsey Settlement. Most of the above had a similar agenda to that of Maude Stanley, whose recommendations deserve close attention.

One of the many major differences between ladies' clubs and working girls' clubs was how potential members joined. In the case of ladies' clubs, if they thought they met the membership criteria, they applied, and were accepted, or, more rarely, rejected. Membership criteria were pretty broad, and in most cases the main obstacle was being able to afford the subscription. However, the procedure in girls' clubs was very different, or at least was supposed to be. Girls were carefully pre-selected, the 'unsuitable' being by implication excluded. This is how, in her book *Clubs for Working Girls*, Maude Stanley advised on setting up a club:

> In starting a club where none has before existed it is sometimes well after taking a room to send invitations for a tea. Let these be given through district visitors, employers, Sunday School teachers of all denominations. After tea let some lady address the girls, tell them what success has attended clubs already established, say what classes will be held, what payment will be required, what amusements will be provided; then, after this address, let the ladies talk individually to the girls, get to know them, get their names and addresses and promises, if possible, of joining the club. It would be well at first starting to ask no admittance fee, but after a month have one of twopence, sixpence or one shilling, and admit all who apply with the understanding that there is no membership till a visit has been paid by a lady to the candidate's home, after which, if satisfactory, a card of membership will be given. It is well to allow girls, once they are members, to introduce other girls. They will be anxious to introduce none but girls who will be a credit to themselves … After a day or two it would be well to call on these girls who gave their names and addresses, and explain more about the club to the girls and to their parents.

Exclusion here is blatant. Only the respectable and deserving are to be invited to join. And even they will be tactfully vetted. As for organising the club:

> We feel a girl's committee could really manage the club entirely alone, but as those who form the committee are all working girls, finishing their work at seven or eight, or later, in the evening, it would be too much to expect of them to give up so much of leisure as would be needed for the whole management of the books, registry of attendances, and payments of club fees. During our superintendent's three weeks' holiday last year the club was managed by the girls' committee, and everything was satisfactory.

So what were these clubs intended to achieve? Refinement was a major item on the agenda. The girls basically needed to be rescued from the presumed vices of their parents' culture, especially gambling, sexual immorality, music halls, and above all the Demon Drink. As Carol Dyhouse pointed out in 1981, girls could not be relied upon to do this without heavy guidance; independence in a girl was to be strongly discouraged:

> It is significant that in most of the literature expounding the need for clubs and societies amongst adolescent girls, the working girl's independence is perceived as 'precocity'. Wage earning is believed to buy them a premature and socially undesirable independence. Further there is a strong assumption ... that financial independence and sexual precocity go hand-in-hand.

Maude Stanley was certainly of this opinion:

> Slowly and gradually the girls have learned that order conduces more to the general wellbeing and comfort than disorder, and that culture and refinement are to a certain extent within their reach. They have realised that their club has been of inestimable value to themselves and that it has given them interests which have brightened their days, that through the club they have found friends who have helped them on in this life and shown them a higher life worth striving for.

This higher life was presumably that lived by Maude Stanley and the circles in which she moved, and if the girls were good and worked hard they might be able to achieve it, 'to a certain extent'. However, it was important that girls did not get above their station. There were definite limits: 'We have not wished to take our girls out of their class, but we have wished to see them ennoble the class to which they belong'. And in fact it was required that a club have at least a good library of approved books, to counteract the effect of the literature that girls would be more likely to come across:

> Books are lent out at many of the low shops at a halfpenny a volume, and so girls as well as boys can get at translations of the worst French novels without difficulty, and once such a taste is got we know what it must lead to.

A similar fear of the effect of cheap literature was expressed by the Snowdrop Bands, whose members promised 'with God's help, to earnestly try, both by our example and influence, to discourage all wrong conversation, light and immodest conduct and the reading of bad and foolish books'.

Still, it was important that workers in girls' clubs should relate positively to the girls; too many of them seem automatically to have slipped into a mistress-servant attitude, which could be resented. As Maude Stanley put it:

Any helper in a girls' club should, above all, have friendliness in her manners and in her heart; to be lively is a great advantage; quietness and decorum are attractive in a girls' club as elsewhere, whereas pride or conceit is soon detected by them. We have heard of girls in a club who openly discussed the ladies who came to them, saying of one, 'We don't like Miss Ann, she is so stuck up! She gives herself such airs!' We need not add that such remarks should never be allowed – not silenced, but, quietly and apart, the girls should be reasoned with.

There could be other difficulties with influential 'helpers':

I have heard of a club where a lady who contributed much of the funds for its maintenance was of such a sensitive organisation that both the playing of the piano and the noise of the games were too much for her; and on her coming into the club everything had to be still. Can we wonder that the girls were often heard to say, 'I won't come to the club tonight if that old cat is there'. … In more than one instance ladies have said to me, 'Our club will not succeed and our old members are leaving because Mrs. Dash is so unpopular with them'. 'Well', I say, 'why do you not get rid of Mrs. Dash?' But unfortunately the lady who is so unpopular may be the important lady of the committee; she may have the purse strings; she may even be the originator of the whole scheme; but her manner is unsympathetic, and commands neither respect nor affection.

Practice

In fact, Maude Stanley's apparently rigorous theory was based firmly on practice, and rigour was often needed. In many clubs the girls were fairly biddable, but in some discipline could be a problem, to put it mildly; when girls turned up the worse for drink and yelling obscenities, no doubt the stereotype of supposed working-class culture was reinforced. The level of discipline, and the way it was maintained, seems to have varied considerably. For instance, in London at the Deptford Fund Girls' Club it was regarded as very important, while at the West Central Club discipline was hardly maintained. At some clubs girls were fined for using bad language. Bright clothes were often deplored, and so often was boisterous, 'unseemly' behaviour, even when there was no bad language or obvious hooliganism. However, attempts to discipline the girls were not necessarily a crude strategy for social control. In some instances the need to 'rescue' girls from potentially harmful behaviour and association could be very real, and even when this was not the case, many girls perceived a social advantage to themselves in adapting their behaviour to the norms expected by the organisers. To quote Iris Dove: 'In certain places it is hard to be clear on the distinction between discipline, protection and empowerment'. And she also makes the point that it is 'important to question whether the clubs imposed

English middle class values on the girls, or whether these were the values to which the girls were aspiring'.

What the girls did in the clubs also seems to have varied; the Soho Club programme, however, seems to have been fairly typical. 'Drill' (i.e. physical exercises) was common to most of them, and regarded as extremely important, but there were other activities and facilities available in all clubs. By the end of the nineteenth century, in Bristol, for example, the Association of Working Girls' Clubs had over 1,240 members in 26 clubs. The clubs all met at least on one or two evenings a week for education and/or recreation. In 1897 the *Englishwoman's Review* reported that in Bristol:

> In nearly all, plain and fancy needlework are taught … [also] drilling and singing classes, cooking, ambulance, basketmaking, leather work. … Although most of the clubs are largely recreational, a few pertain to the nature of evening schools, having classes for reading, writing, arithmetic, geography, drawing and botany. About half the clubs have libraries, the number of volumes they contain varying from thirty to two hundred. Games of all kinds are very general; they give the members great pleasure, affording a wholesome change from the restraint and strain of long hours spent in factory or workroom. Two of the clubs, viz., Norfolk Street and Gaunt House (Orchard Street), open their rooms during the dinner [i.e. lunch] hour in order that girls whose homes are at a distance from their work may have a place of rest and refreshment in lieu of remaining in the factory or walking about the streets. On cold, wet days this is a great boon to the girls, and it is to be wished that the practice of providing such rooms was more general. The Norfolk Street dinner room has a daily attendance of from 700 to 100 girls. It provides conveniences for tea making, and cooking on a small scale. In both places club-workers and friends attend during the dinner hour to entertain the girls with music, singing, recitations or friendly chat.

Also, Maude Stanley notes with approval that girls' clubs in Liverpool and Manchester had baths, which were rather expensive, but the girls seemed happy to pay for their use. Some clubs, such as the Espérance Club and the clubs run from the Women's University Settlement, actually had holiday homes at the seaside or in the country. So it appears that membership of a girls' club could have very practical immediate advantages for working girls, and in the creation of a space where they could find amenities not available to them at work or at home they did begin to resemble women's clubs.

While the intention of many club organisers seems to have been to expose working-class girls to middle-class culture, some organisers came to appreciate the girls' viewpoint and at least modify their stereotype of working-class culture. As the prominent social worker and later even more prominent suffragette Emmeline Pethick put it in 1898, 'There was a time when I thought of working girls as a class. Now I am more inclined to think of young ladies as a class, and of working girls as individuals'. She had been a 'sister' at the West London Mission, and together with Mary Neal had started a club for the working girls of Fitzrovia, who were mainly employed in tailoring and dressmaking – demanding and ill-paid seasonal work. The girls initially seem to have been obstreperous, tearing down gas pipes and breaking furniture, until they were 'quelled' (in Iris Dove's words) by Mary Neal. Soon the club was flourishing, and in 1895 it broke away from the West London Mission, taking a new name of the Espérance Club, indicating the organisers' hope for it and its members. Like other club organisers, they were conscious of the fact that the girls could come under bad influences at home, but they were far more aware of the difficulties rising from the girls' work. As Emmeline Pethick explained,

> The conditions, not only of the home, but of the factory or workshop, had to be taken into account. It became our business to study the industrial question as it affected the girls' employments, the hours, the wages, and the conditions. And we had also to give them a conscious part to take in the battle that is being fought for the workers, and will not be won until it is loyally fought by the workers as well.

This indicates a very different attitude from that of Maude Stanley and other club organisers. Encouraging the girls to take part in the struggle to improve industrial conditions was definitely not part of the usual programme. In fact Mary Neal and Emmeline Pethick started from assumptions that had less to do with those of lady philanthropists than with a dissenting radical tradition of self-help and what would now be called empowerment. They abandoned the settlement-style communal living of the West London Mission and rented a workman's flat so as to live among the people they wanted to help. The activities they especially encouraged were drama, music and dancing, becoming involved particularly with the folk-dance revival of the turn of the twentieth century. Eventually in 1897 the Espérance undertook something quite exceptional for a girls' club: together with some of the older girls, Mary Neal and Emmeline Pethick set up a dressmaking and tailoring business in Great Portland Street which they called Maison Espérance, with working conditions and pay according to trade union recommendations. They also joined with Lily Montagu, who was working with Jewish girls, to set up The Green Lady Hostel, a holiday home for working girls, at Littlehampton. However, Emmeline Pethick met and in 1901 married the rising radical politician Frederick Lawrence, and, as Emmeline Pethick Lawrence found all her energies diverted to women's suffrage. Mary Neal kept on with the club, and developed the folk-dance element to the extent that eventually she was competing with Cecil Sharp; the girls from the club went round the country demonstrating the 'Espérance Morris'. Of course, the Espérance is an extreme example, but it does indicate that all the prescriptive writing about girls' clubs should not necessarily be taken at face value, and that the term 'girls' club' could cover a variety of bodies.

This was also recognised by Lily Montagu, one of the British founders of Liberal Judaism. She had started with a club specifically for Jewish girls, the

West Central Jewish Girls' Club; however, her involvement with the labour movement led her, like Emmeline Pethick, to make a connection between philanthropy and work for industrial improvement, and she became active in the Women's Industrial Council. In this she particularly stressed the need for clubs to help working-class girls both to improve themselves and to organise industrially. With this initial aim she founded the Clubs Industrial Association, and was a leading figure in the movement that culminated in the National Council of Girls' Clubs. However, it should be noted that clubs only attracted a minority of working girls, whether because of the organisers' own principles of exclusion, or because the clubs' relative seriousness tended to deter those who were not seriously 'aspirational'. Money also played a part; many girls could not, or would not, afford even the modest membership charges.

Accommodation

One very important feature of some girls' organisations, most notably the GFS and YWCA, was the provision of safe, affordable residential accommodation for young women. The best known provider of this has been the YWCA, which has run hostels for women since its earliest days. The Mortimer Street hostel was described in 1910 as follows: 'every little cubicle and bedroom has its own window and electric light – there is a wash-room, and a work-room containing provision for heating irons for the use of boarders; the drawing room is kept for reading and music'. The Association's aim was to provide hostels run on modern lines and based on occupants' stated needs. In 1927, it published a booklet *An Ideal Hostel* which recommended the standards of accommodation and service to be offered to residents. By 1960, there were 121 hostels in England and Wales. Four years later, the first Alexandra Residential Club, named after the Association's Vice-Patron, Princess Alexandra, opened in London. It was based on the fruits of consultation with residents and designed to meet the needs of young single people. Other Alexandra Residential Clubs followed in Birmingham, Croydon, Harlow and other places. In 1985, the old style hostels, with accommodation and meals provided, were deemed inappropriate and the Association began to replace them with flatlets. Helen Graham House, opposite the British Museum in Great Russell Street, was opened with 289 places. In another initiative in 1982, the Association's accommodation and advisory service helped more than 2,000 women in London and later continued to operate independently under the title Women's Link.

The First World War and after

The War had a considerable effect on girls' organisations. First, many threw themselves into war-related work – for example the YWCA. When the War began, its main immediate task was to arrange passage for women from belligerent countries who were in England to be safely repatriated. It also provided a club for the many Belgian refugees who had fled to Britain following the German invasion. An Emergency Committee was formed to provide employment for working girls who had lost their jobs because of the war. There was a pressing need for clubs in military centres: 57 Blue Triangle Clubs were opened in the first year of hostilities and there were over 100 by 1918 (the YWCA had adopted the blue triangle as its emblem in 1914). Twenty-nine Centres for Land Girls were also established. On the Western Front in France, the British Government entrusted the spiritual and material needs of the Women's Auxiliary Army Corps to the YWCA. There were also centres for army nurses in the Far East. When the United States entered the war, their government asked the Association to supervise women clerks and nurses at the Front. The Association was equally active during the Second World War, and also opened hostels for war workers and munition workers. At the same time, there was a large increase in mixed youth club membership.

But the real shift seems to have come about after the First World War. There appears to be a marked change in the attitudes of many girls' club organisers, who demonstrate increasingly less confidence in the desirability of imposing refined values on the girls, and more concern with what the girls actually wanted. Also, the type of organiser changed. To quote Madeline Rooff:

> The modern leader emphasises the more positive contributions of club life and sees the constructive value of recreational activities … Many clubs and fellowships are run almost entirely by young people … the elderly officers of the past have given place to young men and women in their early twenties.

This was by no means always uncontested. For example, the Christian Alliance of Women and Girls was a new group which broke away from the YWCA in 1920. It approved of organised games, sports, musical and other drill, but disapproved of 'such secular amusements as dancing, card playing, smoking and theatricals'. Dancing in particular caused much concern, all the more so because it increasingly implied boys – which is another matter, to be considered later.

By the inter-war period, most girls' clubs came, in one way or another, under the aegis of the National Organisation of Girls' Clubs (established in 1909, and from 1926 named National Council of Girls' Clubs). The NCGC did not affiliate individual clubs but worked through national societies and area federations or unions. In 1935 it co-ordinated its efforts with five national societies: the Federation of Working Girls' Clubs, GFS, Girls' Guildry, Girls' Life Brigade and YWCA. These represented over 4,000 clubs in England and Wales, with a total membership of approximately 271,000. The NCGC also had club camps at Filey and Bognor, and an employment bureau for club leaders. Its magazine was *The Signpost*.

Post-war clubs and organisations

In addition to the YWCA and the GFS, there were of course many other clubs and associations. The following are some of the most prominent.

The Federation of Working Girls' Clubs was established in 1887; its motto was: 'By love, serve', and its emblem was a columbine. It was interdenominational, and sought 'to promote the educational, industrial, social, and spiritual welfare of its members'. By 1935 it represented 169 clubs with about 14,000 members, mainly in London and the Home Counties. Together with the NCGC it published the *Girls' Club Journal*. Another organisation, The Girls' Guildry, formed in Glasgow in 1900, continued to be based in Scotland, and was emphatically Christian: its object was 'to help girls to be followers of the Lord Jesus Christ'. Members wore uniform, with decorations for good service, and practised infantry drill. Activities sponsored included training in nursing and health topics, handicrafts, and camp holidays. A similar body, The Girls' Life Brigade, was formed in 1902 under the auspices of the National Sunday School Union, with the motto: 'To save life'. Again, it was uncompromisingly Christian: 'The movement is an integral part of the Church of Christ – not an outside interest'. It was interdenominational, but members were mainly Free Church worshippers. It also strongly supported temperance. In 1935 it had about 940 companies; in England and Wales membership was over 40,000.

There were also other organisations not affiliated to the NCGC; for example, the Catholic Women's League was developing girls' clubs by the inter-war period. However, a much greater impact was made by the Camp Fire Girls. This movement was started in the USA in 1912; in Britain by the 1930s it had 157 Camp Fire Groups and 44 Junior Groups, known as 'Bluebirds'. Most groups were attached to churches. In some ways it resembled such mixed organisations as the Kibbo Kift, the Co-op Children's Circles and the Woodland Folk, since it emphasised camping and 'woodcraft lore', and, also like the Scout and Guide movements, had identifying marks and ceremonies rather opaque to outsiders; for example, its motto was 'Wohelo', which stood for 'Work, Health, Love'. It was also hierarchical; its ranks were, in ascending order, Runners, Fire-makers, and Torch-bearers. There was a uniform, and a ceremonial gown 'like a Red Indian's robe' (with moccasins and fringes). It was strong on ceremonies: 'symbol and ritual play a large part in the weekly programme'. Its aim was

> to give the girl a good time, and while so doing, to help her to realise that woman has a distinctive part to play in the world, and to help her so to develop her personality that she may make the best possible contribution to the life of the home, the nation and the world.

Much later, the noted social worker and political activist Margaret Simey recalled that in the Camp Fire movement,

> we put all the lights out and we drew the curtains, and you dressed up in your Indian stuff with the head band and everything, and you lit a candle, and you recited verses from *Hiawatha*. And I can see the contrast, it must have been wonderful. Now I laugh at it. But on the other hand we worked for badges and things, just like Guides.

Figure 6.3 First Bollington Girl Guide Company in camp, probably 1910. The
Company started as Girl Scouts the previous year

Interestingly, Margaret Simey was a member of the Camp Fire Group led by
Elsie Oxenham, author of the popular Abbey School series of girls' school stories.

And of course it is impossible not to mention the Girl Guides. Immediately
on the founding of the Boy Scouts by Robert Baden-Powell ('B-P') in 1907–8,
there was an eager movement for a girls' equivalent. This seems to have
disconcerted B-P, who was always unsure what to make of women, as is apparent
for example in his book *Rovering to Success*, where he pronounced that as a young
man paddles his canoe throughout life, he must beware of certain rocks on his
way, namely, horses, wine, women, cuckoos and irreligion. Hence he was
reluctant to have anything to do with girls. However, his sister Agnes took the
matter in hand, and in 1910 the Girl Guides were established. The name was
partly a concession to B-P, who disliked the term 'Girl Scouts', although it had
been used already by some independent groups; his reasons were that parents
might be alarmed at the idea, and that the Boy Scouts would see it as an
infringement of their territory. The term 'Guides' was seen as being less
challenging to the general public, while for the more informed it recalled the
Indian Corps of Guides, who 'are distinguished for their general handiness and
resourcefulness under difficulties, and their keenness and courage'. The detailed
history of the Guides is outside the scope of this work, and in any case it can be
found elsewhere. Suffice it to say that for at least 50 years after its foundation it,
together with its junior branch, the Brownies, was extremely popular, especially
among girls of the lower-middle class, and the 'aspirational' working class, though

its membership was (and is) inclusive of all groups, races and classes, including the highest. Before and during the Second World War Princess (later Queen) Elizabeth and Princess Margaret Rose were photographed wearing their Guide/Brownie uniforms. By 1933–4 in England and Wales there were approximately 252,000 Guides, 163,000 Brownies, and over 50,000 Rangers.

By the 1930s, the question of work mobility and consequent feelings of isolation were also regarded as important. As already noted, the YWCA and the GFS provided accommodation, but there was a need for those who did have independent lodgings to find a means for meeting people, and not just other girls. An instance of provision for this is the Wayfarers' Sunday Association, which was founded in 1928, mainly for girls away from home, and mainly based in London. Members made a promise 'to help lonely people and to Keep the Rule', a quotation from St. Paul's *First Letter to the Corinthians,* chapter XIII. Only girls might be enrolled as members, at an extremely modest fee of threepence a month, but they might introduce boy friends. It was open every Sunday from 3.30 p.m. to 9.30 p.m. A typical programme would run approximately as follows: dance music; tea, tea, music and dancing; games; community singing, five-minutes talk and gym; supper, music.

However, most girls' clubs were by the 1930s running into real problems. One was the relative inability of many of them to attract 'the rougher type of girl', a complaint going back to the early years of the clubs, but becoming more pronounced in the inter-war years. Another more serious problem was that the traditional type of girls' club no longer had the same appeal for the older working girls for whom it had been originally designed. As The London Girls' Club Union, founded by Maude Stanley, put it, there was a falling-off after the age of 14. 'The developed girl, about 15 years old, seeks more companionship with boys than can be given at the club'. Even Girl Guides were having problems in this area. According to Madeline Rooff's 1935 report,

> The patrol system, encouraging working in small groups, is ideally suited to the girl of school age. But there comes a time, usually after the girl has gone out to work, or when she has a boy friend, when she is self-conscious in her uniform and Guide activities have no longer the same appeal.

Apart from boys, there were by the 1920s and 1930s far more attractions available to working-class girls. Cinemas and dance halls were obvious examples; even in depressed and impoverished South Wales, where some girls could not even afford to join netball and hockey clubs, it was reckoned that most boys and girls managed to spend at least one or two evenings at the cinema. Also, in 1935 club organisers in Norwich noted that 'new swimming pools with dance floors and restaurants are also springing up, where it is feared that supervision is not always adequate'. Cheap dance halls, with entrance fees as low as threepence, were regarded as a form of bad moral influence which many clubs strove to counteract. To do this, they extended their activities, as already noted, to include not only dancing, and the admission of boys, but cycling, camping and swimming, where facilities existed, in addition to the traditional club libraries and self-improvement classes. But even here they were being marginalised both by local authority educational provision and the activities of such bodies as the Workers' Educational Association, while those older girls interested in swimming, gymnastics and general 'keep fit' (no longer 'drill') activities would be more attracted to something like the Women's League of Health and Beauty, already mentioned in Chapter 5, which was at the apex of its popularity in the late 1930s.

Thus, by the late 1930s, traditional girls' clubs were already under considerable pressure. In the inter-war period they added to their concern for moral welfare and sexual purity an even greater emphasis on motherhood, in keeping with the semi-eugenic concerns of the time. However, they were now competing with a range of activities that were less restrictive and that put much less emphasis on domesticity, and girls were increasingly joining mixed clubs.

After 1945

The social changes associated with the Second World War and its aftermath effectively saw the end of girls' clubs. There had been an increasing move away from single-sex clubs to 'youth clubs', a process that was all but complete by 1950. The YWCA and GFS in particular were compelled to reassess many of their practices. Whereas previously much of the YWCA's activities were based on the provision of meeting places and accommodation the emphasis increasingly became focused on working in the community. Detached youth work, as distinct from youth clubs, was started in Spitalfields, London, in 1965. 'Getwise' courses for 16 to 19-year-old women apprentices and trainees in traditionally male industries were introduced in 1981, and in the 1990s home-based area staff teams of liaison officers specialising in housing or youth and community work replaced regional secretaries. The Association was active in campaigns such as the prevention of violence against women and the need to rid third world countries of debt. Evidence of this shift in emphasis was made clear in the Association's new constitution which came into operation in 1996. Its last purpose built housing project, Bethany House, Exeter, was opened in 1997. By the turn of the millennium, the first transfer of housing stock from the YWCA to other charitable registered social landlords had taken place. Similarly, the GFS revised its procedures. At the time of writing it is known as GFS Platform . It consists of Townsend Fellowships for 15 to 30-year-olds, with 107 branches in England and Wales in 29 dioceses, and in 23 countries worldwide. It runs four Community Projects in Skegness, Penge, Sandown Bay, Isle of Wight and Great Yarmouth. The latter, for example, aims to reduce teenage conceptions among the under-18s, to get more teenage parents into education, training and employment, and to reduce their risk of long-term social exclusion. The Society has long continued to support housing and hostels around the country, but this work is now being transferred to other providers. In December 2002 the headquarters of GFS Platform moved from South Kensington to premises in the City of London.

Some other individual girls' clubs, such as Miriam Moses' Brady Street Club in East London, with its specifically Jewish orientation, continued well into the 1970s, and there are still initiatives towards the formation of girls' clubs in the twenty-first century, but it must be acknowledged that these are exceptional.

So girls' clubs of the traditional pattern, it appears, had served their purpose. And yet in their heyday, from the 1880s to the 1930s, despite their agendas for social control, and all their more obvious failings, these clubs had often in their own way provided a space for working girls that was neither the home, the workplace or the street – a space that was safe, and where to be female was not to be at a disadvantage. And of course other groups for girls continue to flourish, not least the Guides and Brownies. In 2005 Girlguiding UK had a membership of 620,000, and claimed that 30 per cent of all eight-year-old girls in Britain were Brownies. Girls are still learning to claim their own space.

Major sources for this chapter

In addition to organisational publications by, and archives of, the YWCA, the GFS, and Girlguiding UK, there are three major sources: Maude Stanley's *Clubs for Working Girls*, Madeline Rooff's *Youth and Leisure*, and Iris Dove's *Sisterhood or Surveillance?*. Carol Dyhouse's *Girls Growing Up in Late Victorian and Edwardian England* also has some useful insights, as has Brian Harrison's *For Church, Queen and Family*.

Resources for information on the Girl Guides are plentiful. Possibly the most useful are Rose Kerr's *Story of the Girl Guides* and Vronwyn Thompson's *1910...And Then?* as well as the Guides' Annual Reports. Also anything by or about anybody bearing the name Baden-Powell may be illuminating (see the Bibliography).

The YWCA still holds its own archives, as does Girlguiding UK; the GFS archives are available to researchers at The Women's Library.

7   Guilds and institutes

So far the type of association we have dealt with has been the club – a single unit, usually based in a city, preserving its own individual autonomy even when associated with an umbrella organisation such as the National Council of Girls' Clubs or the Working Men's Club and Institute Union and, in many cases where women are specifically concerned, attracting mainly either the well-off or professionals. However, there are three bodies which we think deserve discussion in this context: although not clubs in any real sense, they have served a similar function of bringing together for social, intellectual and political purposes women whose circumstances lie outside those of typical club members. They are the Women's Co-operative Guild, the National Federation of Women's Institutes, and the National Union of Townswomen's Guilds.

The Women's Co-operative Guild

The main activities of the Women's Co-operative Guild (WCG) are somewhat tangential to the concerns of this book, since they were not in the first instance about social interaction, let alone leisure. Nevertheless, its influence and its composition have real significance for the development of a social space for working-class women. Its origins were in the philanthropic impetus of a few women co-operators of more or less academic background. However, it came to be a vocal champion of working-class women's causes, drawing its membership largely from married women – and for these women, leisure was definitely an issue. Leisure for women in the nineteenth century, especially for women of the working classes, was generally seen as problematic, if not undesirable. A woman's work was, in theory at least, never done. Women were supposed to be constantly busy, whether married or single, perhaps working to supplement the family wage, but definitely working hard in the home. The suffragist, writer and Guildswoman Evelyn Sharp recollected her childhood in the 1870s and 1880s, when

> it was unheard of … for a woman's hand to be idle. My own aunt used to keep a half-knitted sock near the front door, so that, if a knock came, she could catch it up and open the door looking as though she had been interrupted in the middle of her work.

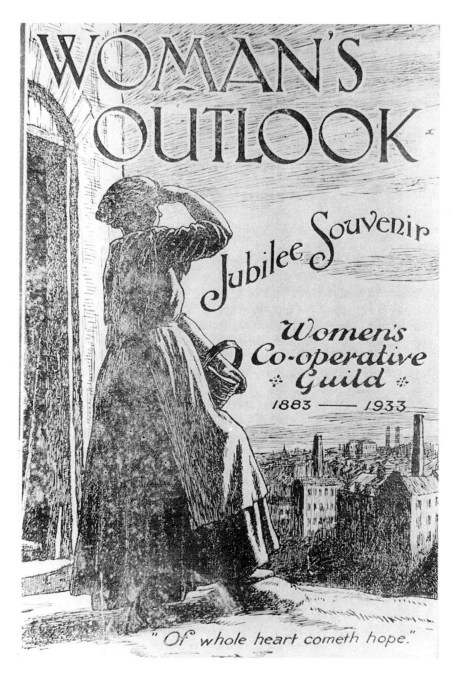

Figure 7.1 Jubilee souvenir of the Women's Co-operative Guild, 1933

Even young women of well-to-do families were encouraged to spend their time on good works, visiting the poor and the like, as well as a great deal of 'make-work' like embroidery. Working-class women had no need to go to these lengths. Real work was always being found for them to do, while their menfolk on the contrary were seen as being entitled to their leisure, whether sporting or in the pub or club, or even the library. In the cities, although for many people poverty was becoming less oppressive, this brought its own problems; as the wages of men especially of the artisan class rose, so did their social expectations. It allowed wage-earning men to aspire to a more 'middle-class' lifestyle. It became a matter of status and pride for a man to be the sole breadwinner, and keep his wife as a full-time housewife, depriving her of any form of social interaction other than the domestic. For many women in the late nineteenth century a social life not centred on the home and family was inconceivable. To quote Evelyn Sharp again, 'the wife of the wage-earning workman had no recognised rights of her own, no independence and no cultural leisure'. And this was particularly true of rural women.

Of course, this was the theory. In practice, as will be apparent from previous chapters, even by the 1880s increasing numbers of women were staking out their social space and claiming their right to leisure, cultural or otherwise, especially by joining clubs. But this was not a realistic option for most working-class women. Quite apart from the cultural expectation that they would be perpetually at work in the home, there were other practical considerations, not least financial. As noted above, members of women's clubs were often well-to-do, or even rich; and those that were not usually came from the professional and intellectual strata, with networks of family or peer support that could be called on. This obviously was not the case with married working-class women. However, there was one area where many women did become involved in matters not directly concerned with the home. Just as with their more prosperous sisters, this was shopping, albeit in this instance not West End shopping for luxuries. This shopping was for everyday necessities, particularly food. And in this a major part was played by the Co-op.

By the 1880s the Co-operative movement was well established in Britain. Although its supporters, who by no means all came from the working classes, were involved in many types of co-operative endeavour, including production co-operatives, its most visible and popular manifestation was consumer co-operation: above all the local Co-operative societies and their stores (the 'Co-op'), retail outlets supplied mainly by the Co-operative Wholesale Society (CWS). These shops distributed profits to their members by means of a 'dividend' paid to individual shoppers, the amount received depending on how much the shopper had paid – a system with only a passing similarity to present-day super-market loyalty card schemes. This, together with the fact that Co-operative prices tended in any case to be lower than other stores, made membership of a Co-operative society very attractive to working-class and lower-middle-class families, and the Co-op remained a popular institution until the later twentieth century.

But the Co-op was not the whole story. Co-operation was much more than just a shopping scheme; it was a movement with strong political and social implications, and close connections with the labour movement, and by 1919 its own political party. It was generally regulated from Manchester by the Co-operative Union, whose paper *Co-operative News* was widely read. In January 1883 the paper started a new venture: a 'Women's Corner', written by Alice Acland, the wife of an Oxford University Extension lecturer and future cabinet minister. This column obviously met a need, and continued to appear in *Co-operative News* for many decades. One of Alice Acland's aims was to extend the co-operative outlook 'beyond retailing', and indeed to raise topics of particular significance to its female readers. A question she posed was, 'What I want to know is – why are we held in such little esteem by men?' She also suggested a 'Women's League for the Spread of Co-operation'. She was soon joined by Mary Lawrenson, a schoolteacher, whose father was a Woolwich printer, and a keen union man. She became the secretary of what was eventually named the Women's Co-operative Guild.

The Guild got off to a slow start. Its first formal meeting took place in May 1883, and by the end of the year it had branches in Hebden Bridge, Rochdale, Coventry, Woolwich, Norwood and Chelsea, with a total of 195 members. Despite the Co-operative movement's northern roots, initially the Guild was stronger in the south of England. However, by the end of the decade, membership had risen to 1,800 in 51 branches, and by 1920 to 51,000 in over 1,000 branches. At first there was a degree of suspicion, not to say hostility, towards an independent women's organisation, and by no means only from men; at an Edinburgh meeting in 1883 it was urged that there should be 'no platform speaking, no advertising, no going out of our women's place'. It is interesting to note that a century after La Belle Assemblée, women's public speaking was still a contentious issue. However, the Guild gained the support of the Co-operative Union, which was important not only as giving it respectability within the movement, but because of the grants it obtained both from the Union and the CWS – though as will be seen, the Guild insisted on its own autonomy. A major development occurred in 1889, when Margaret Llewelyn Davies succeeded Mary Lawrenson as secretary, a post she held till her retirement in 1921.

Like Alice Acland, Margaret Llewelyn Davies was from an academic family. She was the niece of Emily Davies, the founder of Girton College, and her brothers associated with Bertrand Russell at Cambridge. She was in fact acutely aware that this was not typical of most Guildswomen, and was emphatic that women like herself who came from relatively privileged backgrounds should not seek to impose their agenda on the Guild *de haut en bas*, but had to be on equal terms with the other members, and identify themselves with workers' interests. They should act as interpreters of the needs and wishes of working-class women. Indeed, working-class women played an increasing role at all levels in the Guild, although women of wealthier backgrounds, like Virginia Woolf, continued to be attracted to it.

From its beginnings the Guild encouraged discussions, which initially were often of a practical and even domestic nature. The early topics raised tended to show women flexing their consumer muscles, with some criticism of the price and quality of some goods in Co-operative shops which was an example of what came to be called 'basket power'. The Guild never lost its connection with women's interests as consumers, and the symbol most associated with it was the image of the 'woman with the basket'. Still, before long, and especially with the encouragement of Margaret Llewelyn Davies, a far wider range of subjects was discussed. The Guild's 1895 Winter Circular lists, among other things, talks on women's work in local government, women as factory inspectors, women and labour legislation, women as Poor Law Guardians, technical education for girls and women's suffrage. However, not everybody was happy with this last topic. Margaret Llewelyn Davies noted that suffrage was barred from discussion by one or two branches, and she had heard of occasional women walking out when it was decided to read a paper on the 'White Slave' traffic in women and children. On a more prosaic level, the Guild's Annual Report for 1890 notes members' distaste for 'what they consider to be "dull and dry". We have to face the fact that Co-operation and all economic subjects are difficult and require thought and attention'.

Nonetheless, enough Guildswomen found the topics discussed interesting enough to make them want to do more than talk about them, and the Guild began to take on a marked political stance, albeit one that was sometimes contested within its own ranks. This began to bring it into conflict with the wider Co-operative movement. In 1896 a survey of 169 Co-operative Societies conducted by the textile worker and labour activist Sarah Reddish revealed the uncomfortable fact that many women employed by the societies worked inordinately long hours for low pay, and this began a campaign for equal pay within the Co-operative movement, eventually resulting in a minimum wage for Co-operative Societies being introduced in 1907, and in 1912 the CWS, yielding to Guild pressure, resolved to put all its women workers on trade union rates of pay. The Co-operative Union's United Board was also unhappy about aspects of the Guild's anti-credit policy, and especially disapproved of its support, however qualified, for women's votes. The Guild did support the official line that the aim was universal adult franchise; however, it saw women's franchise as being a stepping-stone towards this, rather than a stumbling block on the way.

But the first serious clash came over the Royal Commission on Divorce Law Reform, established by the government in 1909, and to which the Guild gave evidence. The Commission's report was published in 1912, and this led to an outcry within the Co-operative movement, partly at the nature of the Guild's evidence, but also at the fact that it had submitted evidence at all. This was above all the position of the Lancashire Catholic associations, who threatened to tell Catholic co-operators to withdraw funds unless the Guild gave up its work 'in this direction'. The Guild, asserting its autonomy, refused, and from 1914 to 1918 the Co-operative Union withdrew its £400 grant; the Guild immediately established an Independence Fund, but this was still a blow, and there were difficulties financing the Guild's work on maternity. Even so, in 1915 it did manage to get published *Maternity: letters from working women*, which continues to serve as a major source for social history. A later collection of extracts from letters was published in 1931, with a foreword by Virginia Woolf, under the title *Life As We Have Known It*.

By 1918 the Union's grant was reinstated, and the first women's suffrage measure was passed, but there were more conflicts to come, especially between 1921 and 1937, during the secretaryship of Eleanor Barton, when the Guild tended to take on controversial causes, such as support for the peace movement, and held discussions of birth control and abortion that aroused heated passions within the Guild itself, quite apart from incurring the hostility, not only of the Catholic Church (which was predictable) but also of the labour movement (which was less so). However, after the Second World War it lost its controversial reputation, and found itself also losing much of its autonomy, to the extent that in 1964 it consented to a change of name: from 'The Women's Co-operative Guild' it became 'The Co-operative Women's Guild'. In the twenty-first century it seems to have become almost inactive nationally, although local groups continue mainly educational work.

The Women's Co-operative Guild was a political organisation that campaigned both for the Co-operative movement and for the more general women's cause. It was not intended to be a centre for social activities, or even a forum for women's discussion. Despite this, and despite the fact that it began with a philanthropic emphasis, it did provide working-class women with a space that they could call their own, to meet and discuss, and one which was under their own control. The same could be said for the other two organisations in this chapter; but they differ considerably in a number of ways and have more in common with traditional women's clubs.

The Women's Institutes

The Women's Institutes (WI) also had connections with co-operation. Indeed, when they were established in Britain it was suggested that they should be called Women's Co-operative Institutes, a move that was resisted vigorously both by the new Institute members and the Women's Co-operative Guild because of the risk of confusion with the latter.

The position of rural women of the working classes in the late nineteenth century was superficially different from that of town women, especially in industrial areas. Nevertheless, they had more in common than is sometimes supposed. Everything that has been said above about women's work never being done applies at least equally to country women, and not just to wives of agricultural labourers, who were generally recognised at this time to be among the most depressed of workers; wives of smallholders and tenant farmers possibly had if anything an even harder time, since they were often expected to help out with the farm work as well as doing all the housework. On the rare occasions when rural women did find leisure time, their opportunities for relaxation and

120   HOME AND COUNTRY   *June, 1923*

SOME NOTES FROM A VISITOR TO THE N.F.W.I. ANNUAL MEETING.

I VENTURE to send some general impressions of this wonderful gathering. The chairmanship was masterly, clarity, brevity and wit ruled the decisions. Unfortunately the chairman's back was turned to me and the determination and energy expressed by that back cannot be pictured by my fountain pen.

The organisation of the meeting was perfect, the audience was the best behaved that it has ever been my lot to view. The General Secretary on whom the chief responsibility of carrying out the work of Headquarters must rest has a very clever head on very youthful shoulders. The shake of her head as she advised the chairman suggested the wisdom of a Socrates. Alas that I was not seated in the front of the house!

The speaking was excellent. The agenda reflected the intrepid spirit of the Executive Committee. I mastered with difficulty the alternative schemes for a suggested new constitution drawn up by this Committee and three or four points would have raised nice discussions in which I longed to hear the delegates state divergent opinions. My hopes were disappointed, the ladies burked the fences. Conservative woman ruled no change until a change is inevitable. The speakers interested me. They had studied the subjects on which they spoke, they wasted no words, they obeyed the rules as laid down for speakers. The docility of these women to the rule of other women amazed me. The audience interested me even more than the speakers. Never before had I seen such a collection of

Our President.

A W.I. Secretary.

Another President.

Worried W.I. Official.

Strong on Procedure.

women, handsome and plain, old and young, fashionable and staid, but all keen members of the great association which it is evident is setting an

Feather-headed Member.

The Jolly Member.

example of good order and progress to other associations less happily constituted. Adam was banished from this new Paradise where the Eves of many shades and conditions are determined to manage their own affairs. We poor men may look over the garden fence and hope that on a future day, Jill may ask Jack's help in fetching the pail of water.

Future M.P.

The Earnest Member.

I made hasty sketches of some members of the audience to which a kind friend, an ardent Institute member, has put titles. I bought a copy of the little magazine with a geographical cover and amused myself by picking out the typical editor. My friend says it is a speaking likeness.

A Junior Member.

The Editor.

I glanced at the press. One youthful representative appeared almost bored. My prophetic fountain pen pictured him thus in five minutes' time but he wasn't!!

THE PRESS

New Institute Story.

A member's little girl, on being told that Auntie Mary had a new baby said:
"Why, what was the matter with the old one?"

Figure 7.2 Annual general meeting of the National Federation of Women's Institutes as reported in its magazine, *Home and Country*, June 1923

social interaction were even more limited than in the towns. In many villages, in England and Wales at least, most social gatherings available to women were centred on church or chapel, and often subject to a hierarchical control that adult urban women, as distinct from girls, rarely experienced outside the workplace. Thus, the need for centres where women could get together was probably even greater in the country than in towns.

Even so such a movement did not materialise in Britain until 1915, in the middle of a war in which the British government suddenly realised that it had not necessarily been a good idea to let agriculture fade discreetly away. The woman who urged it on the government was actually a Canadian: Margaret Rose Watt, generally known as Mrs Alfred Watt, an activist for the interests of rural women who in 1930 went on to found the Association of Country Women of the World (ACWW). A rural women's institute movement had in fact begun in Canada much earlier, at Stoney Creek, British Columbia, in 1897, with the local Women's Co-operative Institute, as it was called. The Canadian government had been more concerned with agriculture than the British, and possibly more alive to the specific needs of country women, and sponsored this movement.

So after much labour and persuasion, in 1915 Mrs Watt at last convinced the Agricultural Organisation Society to begin setting up Women's Institutes in the countryside; the first such Institute was in Wales, but Sussex soon followed and the movement took off rapidly thereafter. At the time it was seen by government as definitely part of the war effort, to increase agricultural production and reduce dependency on food imports. This was not necessarily the way women saw it. From the outset the stress had been on women's independence and self-reliance, with a strong democratic programme, admittedly urged from above, and at last rural women were finding a space where they could get together. Still, at this time it was still very much under government control; the government agency in 1917 that took over from the Agricultural Organisation Society was now the Board of Agriculture. The woman who was put in charge of the WI was one Gertrude Denman, wife of the third Baron Denman, a former governor-general of Australia, who was obviously regarded as a safe pair of hands. This may have been a mistake from their point of view, although by no means from that of the WI, who still celebrate Lady Denman's memory (despite their vaunted democratic principles, the WI has until comparatively recently had a fondness for titled ladies). To help women who may have been unused to starting and operating groups of this nature, at an early stage the post of Voluntary County Organiser (VCO) was introduced. The VCO's main responsibility was not only to assist with the formation and support of new Institutes, but also for publicity for existing ones. Some of the women involved both as VCOs and as local Institute officials were well known in other spheres: prominent figures like the artist May Morris, daughter of William; the actress and writer Elizabeth Robins; the proprietor of *Time and Tide* Lady Rhondda; and the writers E.M. Delafield, author of the *Diary of a Provincial Lady*, and Virginia Woolf (again!). Although autonomous, the Institutes nationally were represented by the National Federation of Women's Institutes, which gradually took over as government-sponsored bodies withdrew. Its periodical since 1919 has been *Home and Country*, the first editor of which was Alice Williams.

Initially the WI was seen as above all helping the agricultural effort. The original aims and objectives were to stimulate interest in the agricultural industry;

to develop co-operative industries; to encourage home and local industries; to study home economics; and finally, to provide a centre for educational and social intercourse and for all local activities. They were also an attempt to stop a decline in village life, which at an early stage brought them into mild conflict with the Village Clubs Association (VCA), a body started in 1918 with the aim of setting up rural clubs for both men and women, though this body never flourished, and eventually was dissolved. Membership cost two shillings annually for all members, regardless of social class or income, which was one of many attempts, not always successful, to prevent the Lady from the Big House taking control.

By 1918 the WIs were expected to be independent and self-financing, although they did in their early years continue to receive government grants. They were also, unlike such other potential competitors as the Primrose League or the Mothers' Union, explicitly distanced from all political parties and religious denominations. Above all, they were for women, and only women – a point that had to be fought for, and which was not established definitely, and controversially, until the 1923 annual general meeting. Their independence from political parties meant that in the early years they were sometimes accused by the Left of being a prop of the capitalist system; they were supposedly inculcating domestic virtues and unquestioning acceptance of the status quo, and the members were cultural dupes, if not actual crypto-Conservatives. A letter in the January 1924 issue of *Home and Country*, signed 'A Member's Husband', stated that 'in many cases the Women's Institutes are being used as centres of Tory propaganda' by the 'ladies' on Institute Committees 'working very quietly but none the less surely to kill the Democracy of this country and of the movement'. This was vehemently rejected by a wide variety of correspondents, and 'Big Ben' in *Time and Tide* commented sarcastically, 'If the "Democracy" of this country is such a poor thing that it allows itself to die because some of its companions lean towards Toryism, it would be kindness to kill it'. The traditional male Left had already criticised the Women's Institutes along these lines in 1921 in *The Land Worker*, the official organ of the National Union of Agricultural Workers, in an article entitled 'Getting at the Women', which accused them of working 'to counteract the influence of Labour propaganda in country districts'. *Home and Country* retorted that while 'Bolshevism' was not a subject for inclusion in a WI programme, 'Citizenship' certainly was, 'and we do not agree that this title offers an umbrella for anti-Labour propaganda ... The labourer's wife is as important a member as the titled lady'.

Attacks on the WI from the Left are from familiar territory. More unexpectedly the Women's Institutes also came under attack from the Right for their subversive radicalism; again in 1921, a Conservative Association had described the Women's Institutes as a vehicle of Labour propaganda. This may possibly have had something to do with the women-only rule, which caused a great deal of rural male resentment. In Yorkshire, men apparently refused to let their wives join what they called 'a secret society'; as one 'Mere Man' put it in *Home and Country* in 1928, 'I mix with men, many of whom are husbands of Institute members and the things they say about the Institute are unprintable. One told me this morning that damned Institute is the curse of a married man's life'. Generally, the idea that married rural women could have time and space of their own to get together (and presumably compare notes) was felt to be highly challenging, not to say subversive. This was not necessarily something that troubled most WI members; possibly the reverse. As mentioned below, a significant number of them had no problem with confronting established authority, whether that was the authority of the national government or that of rural menfolk. Still, they rapidly secured religious approval; the July 1920 *Home and Country* carried testimonials from the Archbishop of Canterbury, the Catholic Women's League, the National Council of the Evangelical Free Churches, the Chief Rabbi and the Salvation Army. Nevertheless, members were not averse to expressing political opinions, sometimes of a surprising nature; for example, in late 1935 the pages of *Home and Country* hosted a slightly heated correspondence on the Theory of Surplus Value. Certainly, in the 1930s the editorial line of *Home and Country* became increasingly anti-Hitler and anti-Mussolini, despite very occasional letters praising the work these dictators were doing for their countries.

Differing political perceptions of the WI reflect a broader degree of ambiguity in much of its structure and activity. For example, in terms of organisation the Institutes have been a rather ambiguous mixture of top-down and bottom-up approaches which can mislead outsiders, especially those who assume that the general appearance of deference to those in authority means that the WI can be taken for granted, and who are rapidly disabused of this impression. There are numerous examples of this. As well as the notorious slow handclap for Prime Minister Tony Blair in 2000, a less publicised occasion was in the 1980s, when a group allied to the Foreign Office attempted to enlist the WI against the women's peace movement of the time, and got short shrift, since from early on it had been a principle to avoid any activity which could be perceived as preparation for war, or assisting armed conflict (in this at least they had much in common with the Women's Co-operative Guild). As one member put it in *Home and Country* in March 1938, 'War is not a sporadic disease, incapable of eradication, and we, as a non-political body of women, should be prominent in working for its abolition – without which all our social reforms will be futile'.

This became problematic in the Second World War, when the government tried to make the WI do work that could be described as helping the war effort; although Lady Denman was heavily involved with the Land Army, the nearest the WI was prepared to go in this direction was to make more jam for the home market, as well as helping refugees and evacuees and other social relief activities. By New Year 2005 the message seemed to have got through that you do not mess with the WI; at a time when numerous and very vocal Christian campaigners had failed to get *Jerry Springer: the Opera* banned from BBC television, the BBC had already responded to WI pressure by apologetically editing out references from a comedy programme that portrayed WI members as racist and homophobic. The guest speaker at the 2005 annual general meeting was Jane Fonda. Still, despite this non-establishment record, and of course the amusingly irreverent nude calendar that was the inspiration for the film *Calendar Girls*, the

WI members' own view of themselves, as well as that of the media, tends to be of respectability rather than radicalism.

The diffuseness of the different Institutes meant that they could in the mass appear to be all things to all people. Not all political comment was hostile; romantic socialists and conservative landowners could both find much to approve of in them. To most members a strong source of attraction was their independence from the Church, which commended itself especially to nonconformist women, and from the local landowners, which commended itself to the working-class women. Institutes were urged to include 'cottage people', and from the early days it was felt that an Institute that relied mainly on well-to-do women was not a real Institute. Real concern was caused in September 1923 by a letter by 'An Upholder of the Constitution' to *Home and Country* that protested about

> the snobbery existent among the *ladies* (italics please!) of some Women's Institutes …. When tea time comes at the meetings, these *ladies* all sit together and tea is served to them first …. [At a private house] there was a marked difference between the tables set for the great and the small.

Most correspondents indignantly refused to accept that this referred to more than a tiny minority, but 'A Democrat' acknowledged that

> in rural districts where for centuries the 'people' have lived in humble subordination it requires courage to express opinions fearlessly, but a dozen of the humblest members taking counsel together could banish the outward signs of snobbery and work a revolution in the Institute.

She concluded, 'It is in the WI alone that I ever hear now the distinction between "ladies" and "women"'. There have also been other sources of division, not least because the WI ethos appears overwhelmingly English. An extreme reaction to this in 1967 provoked Zonia Bowen, exasperated by monoglot Anglophone WI organisers, to start the Welsh-speaking Merched y Wawr (Daughters of the Dawn). Based in Aberystwyth, it has strong links with the Welsh language and nationalist movements, and is popular in majority Welsh-speaking areas, although the WI also continues to have a marked presence even there.

In the WI, as already noted, party politics have been shunned, and so sometimes have been non-party political issues that could be perceived as potentially divisive, although a rule explicitly barring discussions of this nature was modified as early as 1918. Still, many suffragists became involved in the WI from the outset, and local feminists did not distance themselves, though the WI as a whole never called itself feminist or even, it seems, associated itself with overtly feminist positions. Even so, they soon became involved in campaigns around such issues as health, maternal welfare, child welfare, support for unmarried mothers and other subjects that appear to have at least a tangential feminist connection, but which at the time could simply be regarded as 'social issues'. The WI did, however, identify itself strongly with national issues: not necessarily nationalist ones, but issues of national importance. For example, they campaigned for managed waste disposal in 1925, and for adequate school lunches in 1926. Their motto is 'For Home and Country', although 'Country' is somewhat ambiguous in this connection, as the WI was sometimes referred to as the 'Countrywomen's Parliament' – with some reason, since even by the end of the 1920s the national membership had passed 250,000, and in 2005 it had only fallen to 220,000. At the time of writing, they remain by far Britain's most popular women's organisation, at least in terms of membership. And of course they rapidly became a national institution. It is the only women's organisation that has needed to book London's Royal Albert Hall for its annual general meeting.

So what did (and do) Women's Institutes actually do? A letter to *Home and Country* claimed to have heard it said that 'our Institutes are just groups of women who meet together for tea and a good gossip'. Although this sort of social interaction was not automatically ruled out, it has never been the main purpose of the Institutes. Initially, one of the purposes for which the government supported them was the wartime need for economic self-sufficiency throughout the country, stressing the importance of using local material in the most economical manner. Also, they were expected to provide various sorts of practical education, particularly in the matter of providing food for the nation. At first this had something of the air of well-off ladies telling poor women how to run their kitchens, but it rapidly became more realistic. An especially successful venture in this field was craft training. The initial move to start a WI toy society proved a commercial failure, but more local specialised ventures found a market; for example, the Ticehurst WI produced smocks that were sold at Liberty's; Micheldever WI not only revived the obsolescent skill of rush-making and sedge-making, but thereby produced saleable mats, baskets, chair-bottoms and hats, among other things. Rabbits seem to have been a popular source of raw material; there were especially lectures on rabbit skin curing, and some Institute members made for sale fur gloves from rabbit skins. Elsewhere, WI members made artificial flowers, dolls and toy animals, and of course jam. Jam making had begun during the war as a useful and nutritious way of preserving surplus fruit, and in 1920 the National Federation was finally successful in persuading the government to let it have 50 tons of sugar for 'co-operative jam making' for the use or profit of the Institute as a whole. All these activities could provide a source of income for rural women. In many towns WI Trading Shops were started to sell members' work.

However, craft work could be a source of division. The cult of the rural and the 'folk' was still very potent among the better-off WI members, many of whom deplored the commercial crassness of making artificial flowers and toys. This showed that the spirit of true craft was lacking, and so the purists set up a Guild of Learners, for those who wanted to rediscover the timeless arts of the English Folk, along with the romantic self-sufficiency of Welsh homespun. The Guild of Learners promoted skill in 'traditional' country crafts, and organised competitions, in which working-class women seldom participated, having less time to perfect the 'traditional' skills that were rather exotic to them than the more leisured women. A similar attitude was exhibited to other approved 'folk' activities unknown to the actual folk, like folk dancing, which seems to have been regarded with a wary tolerance; as a correspondent to *Home and Country* commented,

> it was a new kind of dancing called folk dancing which isn't rightly new, but a very old kind, same as they used to dance in the days when they used to call this country Merrie England which must have been a long time ago.

In some Institutes there seems to have been a rather relentless Olde Worlde element, with members being induced to learn 'Strip the Willow' or 'Gathering Peascods' and putting on Elizabethan masques slightly reminiscent of E.F. Benson's *Lucia* books. Still, the craft activities provided a few relatively leisured women the opportunity to do creative non-commercial craft work; it also gave rather more women a chance to engage in women-centred leisure, whatever the shape of the baskets they made.

In fact Institutes have always been involved in a wide range of activities. Whist drives have always been popular, and some Institutes even in early years indulged in non-folk dancing. Amateur dramatics took off early, and although there was strong pressure to stick to Shakespeare, for Christmas 1921 the Hamsey and Cooksbridge Institute in East Sussex staged a *Sleeping Beauty* pantomime. Specifically social meetings seem to have been frequent, with such activities as talks and music, as well as tea. In fine weather, garden fêtes were often arranged, as were sales of work. Attendance at these events in the 1920s seems to have been expected to be over 50, and this could go much higher for special occasions, as when the Newham, Co. Durham, WI threw a New Year 1920 party for school children and old folks, which had an attendance of 140. Parties were common, and sometimes were arranged for fundraising purposes; also in 1920, the Henfield, Sussex, WI held two parties a week in aid of the Save the Children Fund. More seriously, there were debates and discussions, as well as lectures, with topics like pensions for widows, or a debate on whether women workers from the war should resume their pre-war sphere (the motion was resoundingly defeated). Local WI outings were often arranged. For example, between 1934 and 1938 the WI at Layer-de-la-Haye, near Colchester, went to visit a battleship, a London theatre, Windsor, and the Royal Tournament at Earls Court, London; and in 1936 the WI at Barton Stacey, near Andover, Hampshire, organised a coach outing to Bournemouth for members and their children which incidentally revealed how necessary such outings could be to overcome rural isolation: children seeing a policeman thought he was their village policeman, having never seen anybody else wearing that uniform.

The venues for these activities varied. Usually it was a local village hall, or parish hall; it might be a member's house, though this could cause problems; and in some cases, mainly in market towns or county towns, it was a dedicated

Women's Institute Centre. In many ways, these resembled the early provincial women's clubs, since they not only provided a venue for Institute activities, committee meetings, and the like, but often also a rest room, where WI members from out of town could leave parcels, bicycles, and even in at least one case their babies, while they went to the market or the shops, and where they could get a cup of tea and at least a sandwich or a cake before returning home. In most cases, newspapers, both national and local, were provided. Early examples of these Centres were to be found in Dorchester, Ely, Norwich, Newport, Isle of Wight, and Truro. A resident caretaker, sometimes called the Matron, and usually a WI member, was reckoned to be necessary for the running of a Centre, although this was not so necessary if the Centre was only open on market days, like that in Ely, where attendance on Thursdays counted between forty and sixty members. Dorchester, which was open every day, reckoned that 1,200 members had used the rest room alone in 1922. The Newport Centre also had a Handicraft Stall to which members could bring their own work or produce, such as eggs, butter, chutney and (of course) jam for sale, a penny in the shilling being deducted from their takings to cover expenses. The funding of these Centres varied considerably from one location to another. In Dorchester a house was lent by a local gentleman, and the local Institutes each paid £1 1s a week for the Centre's upkeep; while in Newport rooms above a draper's shop were rented for 10s a week, and presumably again local Institutes contributed to its running. Truro was more ambitious. There in 1918 a building formerly used for public baths was purchased for £600, with another £200 being allowed for renovation and repairs. A mortgage was taken out and £800 borrowed; the lenders' lawyer held the mortgage till the debt was paid off, which by diligent fundraising, including hiring rooms for meetings, the Institute was able to do within a few years, henceforward owning the freehold and the structure outright. This meant that in addition to meeting rooms, a rest room, a hall and a resident caretaker, the Centre had a library which by 1923 had about 1,000 books. The hall was used among other things for weekly dancing classes and a monthly dance, in addition to the usual whist, acting, music and choral singing.

Social activities were regarded as an essential part of WI life, and the National Federation of Women's Institutes actually issued a booklet on *The Social Half-hour*. In 1933 VCOs were urged to help WI members realise that the social half-hour was not a dispensable extra to the monthly meeting but an essential feature, and that the half-hour did not mean simply tea and perhaps a display of work done at home. There does seem to have been an awareness that this appeared to be telling women how to enjoy their leisure, since the document acknowledged that there was some blurring of the distinction between 'social' and 'educational' elements in WI activity. Actually, there seems already to have been a fair variety of activities. In 1931 a local WI reported that a meeting started with the singing of *Jerusalem*, continued with a demonstration of home-dyeing, and proceeded to a sketch by members entitled 'Lobster Salad', all of which seemed extremely funny to *Punch*.

But whatever those at the top intended or urged, the actual women who were members of the Institutes decided their own agenda according to their own inclinations, which of course varied according to the location and makeup of individual Institutes. It was a source of concern to the higher-minded WI members that attendance numbers at such social affairs as dances far outstripped those at talks on the future of agriculture or the current economic situation, and inevitably the actual donkey-work of running the Institutes tended to be left to the better-off women. Even so, individual WIs have not been shy of debating controversial issues, from birth control in the 1920s to decriminalising prostitution in the early twenty-first century. Even in the 1920s WIs were not absent from the broader political scene; for example, they collaborated with the National Council of Women in campaigning for women police. They also worked with the Maternity and Child Welfare League, especially in connection with the high-profile inter-war National Baby Week. On a wider front, they supported the League of Nations, and since 1946 have co-operated with the United Nations Association. And, as may be gathered from the above, in the inter-war years many members supported the Women's International League for Peace and Freedom, though more women turned out for campaigns to stop local bus companies raising fares for, or even cutting, services to market towns, as they did for frequent campaigns on housing in rural areas. Getting women onto local councils – Parish Councils, Rural District Councils, County Councils – was also a frequent campaign issue. Even so, the WI does have a distinctly mumsy image: women of middle years more interested in whist drives, cooking and jam making than political or organisational issues, which probably is not too much of a caricature.

Townswomen's Guilds

In the 1920s the success of the Women's Institutes inspired the campaigning feminists Eva Hubback and Margery Corbett-Ashby to try something similar for urban women. Both of these women had been active in the non-militant National Union of Women's Suffrage Societies, and were among the leaders of its successor, the 'new feminist' National Union of Societies for Equal Citizenship; Eva Hubback was editor of its weekly the *Woman's Leader.* The problems they perceived faced by women in towns were somewhat different from those addressed by the WI. Whereas country women needed to make space in their own close and hierarchical communities, urban women were already by the 1920s finding themselves increasingly isolated, as the old street culture was replaced by new well-appointed but anonymous housing estates and suburban sprawl, particularly the ribbon development along arterial roads that was a particular feature of the inter-war period. The need was perceived to be for women in towns to have opportunities first to meet, and then to compare notes, gather information, take civic action and generally to mix socially. The first such body was started in 1929 at a country town, namely Haywards Heath in Sussex, and it was rapidly joined by groups at Burnt Oak (a North-West London suburb),

Moulsecoomb (a suburb of Brighton) and Romsey in Hampshire (an independent country town, but definitely within the orbit of Southampton). By the end of the year, 26 such groups had been formed. At first these were called 'Women's Town Institutes', but after representations from the WI, they were re-named Townswomen's Guilds (TG). By 1931 thirteen federations had been set up to help individual Guilds communicate with each other.

Initially, the Guilds were perceived by the organisers as something of an offshoot of the National Union of Societies for Equal Citizenship. However, a defining moment came in 1932. Since the gaining of equal franchise for women in 1928 and the 'flapper' election of 1929, the Union had been reassessing its function, and decided to divide its activities. The political campaigning would be consigned to a new body called the National Council for Equal Citizenship, while the educational and informative function was to be entrusted to the Townswomen's Guilds, together with the *Woman's Leader* (from 1933 the *Woman's Leader*'s title was changed to *The Townswoman*); thus it was that this paper ended 1931 with articles on the economic crisis and ended 1932 with articles on domestic pets. In that same year a national organisation was formed: the National Union of Townswomen's Guilds, which adopted the colours of the old National Union of Women's Suffrage Societies, namely, red, white and green (the coincidence with the Italian flag and its Risorgimento associations was originally deliberate). On the other hand, the 1932 annual general meeting had eschewed all political propaganda in order to concentrate on the education of women as citizens, indicating a potential overlap with the activity of the National Women Citizens' Association. And, as indicated above, the focus of Townswomen's attention was shifted very much in the direction of the domestic. In the 1930s, the Guilds expanded considerably, so that in 1938 the National Union headquarters finally moved out of its little bungalow in Westminster to more spacious premises in the Cromwell Road. During the Second World War they seem to have had few of the inhibitions of the WI about doing war work at the specific request of the Ministry of Labour, and after the war they received a grant from the Ministry of Education towards their work.

So what is that work? Every Guild holds regular monthly meetings and, in addition, the annual programme includes speakers, demonstrations and social activities. Townswomen get involved in many leisure activities, from line dancing to public speaking, from drama to arts and crafts, from music to sports. Also, since the 1950s, Townswomen have been much less shy about dealing with public issues: issues that are political in the non-party sense, such as support for refugees, concern over divorce and separation and child sexual abuse. But as with the WI, what really attracts most members is the social life. Basically, Townswomen just want to have fun. However, the town is not the country. Women in towns, or even suburbs, have far more opportunity for a social life outside the home and neighbourhood circles than, by and large, do their rural sisters. So the Towns-women's Guilds do not compete in numbers or in influence with the Women's Institutes, though its membership is far from small – about 50,000 at the time of writing, organised into 1,300 Guilds and 111 Federations. It is one of the means by which urban women, usually, be it said, of a certain age and a certain class, can find a social space.

PS: *Jerusalem*

In the early 1920s a tradition grew in many WIs of singing the setting of words by William Blake known as *Jerusalem* at the start of the monthly meeting, and by 1924 it was being sung at the national meetings. Since then *Jerusalem* has become inescapably associated with the Women's Institutes, and to a lesser extent the Townswomen's Guilds. Why is this? There are good historical reasons. Blake's words, which are actually from the preface to his poem *Milton* (the long poem Blake titled *Jerusalem* is very different), had throughout the nineteenth century been adopted by radical and reforming groups; for example, women's suffrage groups frequently used them in their publicity. One of the people to whom the words especially appealed was the composer Hubert Parry, a strong supporter of radical ideas, particularly women's rights. In 1916 he had, together with other prominent people of a liberal disposition such as Gilbert Murray and Evelyn Underhill, joined a group called Fight for Right, and it was for this group that he composed his now famous setting of 'And did those feet …?'. Unfortunately, Fight for Right rapidly developed into a rather intensely patriotic body, so that the liberal element, including Parry, quietly dropped out; and Parry took the tune with him. So, when women won the first instalment of the vote in 1918, Millicent Fawcett, leader of the National Union of Women's Suffrage Societies, asked Parry if he had anything he could contribute to a celebratory concert; Parry produced his *Jerusalem*, which Millicent leapt on with delight, pronouncing it the women voters' hymn. That is the initial reason why many women's organisations, and especially the WI, are so attached to the song.

Major sources for this chapter

We have relied most of all on the periodicals of the three main organisations mentioned: *Co-operative News*, *Woman's Outlook*, *The Townswoman* and especially *Home and Country*. In addition, the following secondary works contain a great deal of useful and interesting information: *Caring and Sharing*, by Jean Gaffin and David Thoms; Margaret Llewelyn Davies' *Life as We Have Known It* and *Maternity*; Evelyn Sharp's *Buyers and Builders*; Maggie Andrews' *The Acceptable Face of Feminism*; Inez Jenkins' and J.W. Robertson's histories of the Women's Institute Movement; Mary Stott's *Organisation Woman*; and Caroline Merz's *After the Vote*.

Information about the history of *Jerusalem* is in J. Dibble's life of Parry. Archives of the National Federation of Women's Institutes are held at The Women's Library, London; papers of the Women's Co-operative Guild/Co-operative Women's Guild are with the Co-operative Union in Manchester; and the Townswomen's Guild maintains its own archive.

8 'Service' clubs

Rotary, Inner Wheel and Soroptimist International

One of the features of American culture that spread worldwide in the twentieth century was the idea of 'service' clubs, acting mainly or wholly to benefit the community. It has already been noted in our chapter on women's clubs that in the nineteenth century such clubs in the USA differed markedly from their British equivalents in this respect. Few British women's clubs saw it as part of their remit to do good works, while this was a central concern of the majority of American women's clubs. However, the twentieth century transatlantic influence in this direction came from a very different source, namely the American project of Rotary Clubs, and their offshoots or imitators, such as the Round Table and the Lions, all of which have international aspects. Despite the fact that until fairly recently Rotary was an uncompromisingly male organisation, from very early on women have either taken part in activities supporting Rotary or have organised themselves along similar lines.

Rotary Clubs

The beginnings of the Rotary Club movement actually seem to have had little to do with service. They were the brainchild of Paul Percival Harris, a Chicago businessman, who had long been troubled by the isolation of businessmen based in the same town but in different lines of business. He suggested that it would be a good idea to bring them together in a club. Since they would not be in direct competition with each other, he saw no reason why they could not become friends, and even more importantly, he considered that they could be of mutual help by putting business in each others' way. The first such club was started in Chicago in 1905 and was an immediate success. At first the name was probably the Booster Club, but it was soon changed to the Rotary Club, either because initially meetings were held in members' homes in rotation, or, as Harris later recalled, the original intention, never carried out, had been to rotate membership. Whatever the facts of the case, rotation in members' homes was very short-lived. Soon the Club was hiring a room at a local hotel, and quickly got the hotel to serve them meals in it. Thus the conventional pattern of Rotary meetings was set, giving rise in 1930 to George Bernard Shaw's famous gibe, 'I can tell where Rotary is going without travelling to Edinburgh to find out. It is going to lunch'. What came to be called the classification system was present from the outset, meaning that there was to be one member from each trade or profession (this has since been modified in various ways). Meetings were first fortnightly, but soon the need was felt to meet weekly. A wheel was adopted as an emblem, although its exact form was not standardised until many years later. The idea rapidly caught on, and soon other US cities had their own Rotary Clubs.

So from the start the Rotary was an instrument for mutual business benefit, with a strong social element: a good solid American institution focussed on the profit motive. Nevertheless, the Chicago Rotary Club soon became involved in what at the time was called 'civic work', its first venture in this area in 1907 being to sponsor the provision of public toilets in downtown Chicago. The balance was thus already shifting by the time that, at the first Rotary Convention in 1910, Arthur Frederick Sheldon proposed the motto: 'He profits most who serves best'. Three years later the Minneapolis Rotary Club went further with 'Service before self'. Since then both these mottoes, but mainly the latter, have been used by the vast majority of Rotary Clubs. In 1911 Harris's own revised definition was that 'Rotary should consist of a national mixture of business with civic activities and good fellowship'. Increasingly, an ethical dimension was being stressed: Rotarians should not just look to make a profit, but should adopt good honest business practice.

In 1911 Rotary reached Dublin, and shortly thereafter Britain, due initially to the efforts of William Stuart Morrow, an Irishman who graduated from Trinity College, Dublin, but who subsequently emigrated to California. When Rotary started in San Francisco in 1908 he became an enthusiastic member, and actively promoted Rotarian ideas. Following a business failure, he returned to Ireland where he continued proselytising for Rotary. He soon took Rotary ideas to Britain, first to Scotland and soon thereafter to England. Meanwhile Arthur Sheldon and his deputy E. Sayer Smith were starting clubs in London and Manchester.

While many British businessmen heartily supported the idea of Rotary, when Morrow among others tried to introduce American-style meetings, he was met with a degree of incomprehension, not to say embarrassment. In Edinburgh particularly prospective Rotarians were more than a little taken aback by the singing between luncheon courses of 'I am a Little Prairie Flower' or 'Old MacDonald's Farm', complete with actions. The practice of addressing all members by their Christian names was flatly rejected; as one Dundee member put it in 1929, some of the fellow members were not only old enough to be his father but solid members of the community, and taking such liberties would be quite offensive. More seriously, the US Rotary culture was very much along 'booster' lines, with plenty of 'stunts': for example, at lunch a member would suddenly be called on to give the names and exact classifications of all others at his table, and would have to pay a forfeit if he failed. Also, a regular feature was to draw at random from a hat the name of the member who was to win the week's 'Boost Prize', meaning that all other members present were expected to take every opportunity to put all the business they could influence in his way for the coming week. This drew a sharp rebuke from the Edinburgh Rotarians, who had obviously taken seriously the rhetoric about 'service before self'. As Roger Levy quoted them,

> While the principle of friendly relationship between business and professional men was not only pleasant but helped at the same time to improve the services which the members were able to render to the public also, the use of the Club to promote the business of individual members was highly undesirable.

The charge of mixing a rhetoric of high principles with a practice of indifferent business ethics is one that has often been levelled at Rotarians by such critics as Dorothy Parker and H.L. Mencken, but most famously by Sinclair Lewis in his novels *Babbitt* and *Elmer Gantry*. In *Babbitt*, published in 1922, Rotary is not named as such, though the 'Booster Club' of Zenith City is an easily penetrable disguise. Five years later, in *Elmer Gantry*, the gloves are off:

> The Rotary Club was an assemblage of accountants, tailors, osteopaths, university-presidents, carpet-manufacturers, advertising men, millinery-dealers, ice-dealers, piano salesmen, laundrymen, and like leaders of public thought, who met weekly for the purposes of lunching together, listening to addresses by visiting actors and by lobbyists against the recognition of Russia, beholding vaudeville teams in eccentric dances, and indulging in passionate rhapsodies about Service and Business Ethics. They asserted that their one desire in their several callings was not to make money but only to serve and benefit a thing called the Public.

The book goes on to demonstrate how little the Rotarians live up to their professed ideals and in passing throws in the suggestion of links to the Ku Klux Klan.

That such criticism may have been somewhat over the top was later recognised even by Lewis, but the idea that Rotary exists mainly as a means of mutual back-scratching still is a sensitive issue for Rotarians, and one that they regularly confront. To take just one example, in Britain in 1969 an advertisement for the General Post Office included the statement: 'Join our Rotary Club, you'll make business contacts faster'. This was met with public indignation from the Rotary International of Great Britain and Ireland who protested against this 'popular misconception'. The charge of racism also arises occasionally, and not only in the land of the Ku Klux Klan. A notorious example occurred in Britain when in 1968 the former Conservative Minister Enoch Powell made a speech to the London Rotary Club's annual conference at Eastbourne denouncing non-white immigration (copies had been carefully distributed to the press in advance) in which he followed up his reference earlier in the year to 'the Roman poet' seeing the River Tiber foaming with much blood. This of course gained much adverse publicity, and Rotary found itself associated with Powell's views. In 1969 RIBI invited John Akar of the Rotary Club of Freetown, Sierra Leone to speak on racial issues to the annual conference at Bournemouth but his speech seems to have been received somewhat coldly. Yet it is important to note that even at the time this attitude did not seem to be widespread, and at least in the twenty-first century racism is not a characteristic usually associated with Rotary, which is a genuinely international movement. Additionally, it should be noted that the authors have found their references to most of the negative criticisms of Rotary quoted from officially approved Rotarian sources. Rotarians appear to be far from immune to self-criticism.

There are two poles to Rotary organisation. On the one hand, Rotary long ago became a formidable international concept, with Rotary Clubs in almost all countries outside the old Communist blocs and perhaps some Islamist nations, and these are all in theory regulated by Rotary International. On the other hand, from earliest days the principle of the autonomy of individual clubs has been stoutly upheld, as for example in the case of Enoch Powell's speech. In between these are the national Rotary organisations, trying to keep Rotary International happy while not interfering in the internal affairs of individual clubs. In Britain the responsible body is the Rotary International of Great Britain and Ireland, usually referred to as RIBI, of which more anon. Despite the criticisms above, and certainly without ruling out the likelihood that connections made at Rotary may be useful in business, at the very least since the 1930s, and in many cases long before, Rotary has been a 'service' organisation in fact as well as name. Unlike some organisations with which it is sometimes compared, like for example Masonic orders (although, like the Masons, Rotarians faced Catholic disapproval from 1929 until the papacy of John XXIII in the late 1950s), Rotary is very outward-looking by nature, and not merely incidentally. As early as 1921 Rotary International had adopted as part of its objects the following:

(a) High ethical standards in business and professions
(b) The ideal of SERVICE as the basis of all worthy enterprise
(c) The active interest of every Rotarian in the civic, commercial, social and moral welfare of the community
(d) The development of broad acquaintanceship as an opportunity for service as well as an aid to success
(e) The interchange of ideas and business methods as a means of increasing the efficiency and usefulness of Rotarians
(f) The recognition of the worthiness of all legitimate occupations and the dignifying of the occupation of each Rotarian as affording him an opportunity to serve society.

Later, Rotary International adopted the 'Four Way Test':

'Of the things we think, say or do:
    Is it the TRUTH?

Is it FAIR to all concerned?
Will it build GOODWILL and BETTER FRIENDSHIPS?
Will it be BENEFICIAL to all concerned?

British Rotarians under the aegis of RIBI have been making their contribution to service for many decades. RIBI became a British national institution surprisingly quickly; the 1921 convention succeeded in obtaining a message of support from King George V, and later that year it was one of a select number of organisations to place a wreath on the tomb of the Unknown Warrior in Westminster Abbey. Later it was active in urging, and obtaining, from individual clubs help for 'distressed areas' and such apparently unlikely bodies as the Miners' Relief Fund; it is seldom realised that some prominent trade union leaders have been Rotarians. After the Second World War they were particularly active both in foreign aid and at home. They raised money for food and clothing for the destitute in Germany, not a popular cause at the time, and eastern Europe, and especially in Greece. In Britain this was the period of providing radio for the bedridden, and particularly of the Rotarian Christmas Tree, which nowadays seems unfortunately to have declined to a loudspeaker van putting out poor quality tapes of carols and a bedraggled Santa with a collecting box. However, other initiatives have not declined in the same way. Local Rotary Clubs appear happy to get involved with fundraising for local needs, and there is no question about the degree of their involvement at a national level. By the 1970s, RIBI-affiliated clubs were helping to fund the Ranfurly scheme for sending library books to countries where they could not be afforded as well as drilling rigs for wells in Africa and Asia, and kidney machines at home. More recently, while it may not be surprising that they raised £6,500,000 for relief for the Christmas 2004 Asian tsunami, to put this in context, just before Christmas they had also donated over £1 million to the cause of children's hospices.

One further, possibly less welcome sign of the times: because of the pressures of twenty-first century business culture, increasingly Rotarians do not go to lunch. Instead, they do breakfast.

Women and Rotary: Venture Clubs and the Inner Wheel

As indicated above, Rotary from the beginning emphatically excluded women. However, since Rotarians were usually businessmen of some standing in their own communities, whose wives were expected at least to play the part of hostess when bosses or colleagues came to dinner, women relatives of Rotarians very soon came to take an active interest in Rotary activities. As the service ethic grew in importance in Rotarianism, so too did the women's interest grow, and some Rotary clubs soon had 'ladies' committees' or 'ladies' auxiliaries' attached. In Britain this development was accelerated by the First World War. For example, in Liverpool in 1917 there was a group calling themselves 'Rotary Ladies' devoted mainly to relief work in connection with Rotary projects. However, the real growth in women's involvement in Britain came after the war, when a number of women's groups were formed which were more or less connected with Rotary. An early and important one was the Venture Club of Bristol, started in June 1920. It stated in its constitution that to be eligible for membership the woman must be a proprietor, partner, director or manager of a company doing legitimate business in the Bristol area. A service committee was appointed and their first project in 1921 was to befriend motherless girls. The Bristol area was also a focus of Rotary activity, including especially substantial support for the creation of the Bristol Little Theatre and the establishment of a Boys' House at Weston-Super-Mare to provide holidays for children from deprived backgrounds. Incidentally, however, the ongoing drain on resources that the latter involved was a factor in persuading Rotary Clubs henceforward to make one-off or at least fixed-term donations, rather than open-ended commitments.

The Venture Club had been running successfully for three years without attracting too much notice until 1923, when an open letter was sent to RIBI urging recognition of Women's Rotary Clubs, of which a few were already in unofficial existence, and which were known like the pioneer in this respect as Venture Clubs. Signatories to this letter included such very prominent names as those of Lady Rhondda, feminist campaigner and editor of *Time and Tide*; the Anglican preacher and campaigning feminist Maud Royden; and the two first women Members of Parliament, Lady Astor and Mrs Wintringham. This proposal was emphatically turned down by RIBI, and the women involved set about forming their own Provisional Club in London in 1924. At the same time Stuart Morrow, the indefatigable promoter of service clubs, had introduced the concept of Soroptimist Clubs to Britain, and eventually the members of the Provisional Club and the Venture Clubs became Soroptimists, of which more below. The official position of both Rotary International and RIBI was then and remained until 1987 that women could not be part of a Rotary organisation; indeed Rotary International has until relatively recently tended to uphold the idea that women can have no connection with Rotary at all, but RIBI has been rather more flexible on the issue, which was just as well, because during the 1920s there were various initiatives involving women in Rotarian activities. These included the Bexhill Women's Wheel of Service (1924), and Ladies' Auxiliaries at Southend-on-Sea (1924), Canterbury (1925), Clapham, Guildford and Littlehampton (1926), Colchester (1927), Woolwich (1928) and Brixton, Chatham and Sunderland (1929).

The initiative that was eventually the most successful in Rotarian terms, however, took place in Manchester. On 15 November 1923 a meeting of Rotarian wives was called by a Mrs Oliver (Margarette) Golding, formerly a nurse, but by then managing director of a nurses' outfitting company in Stockport, near Manchester. The meeting took place in the cooling room at Herriot's Turkish Baths on Deansgate. The reason for this slightly unorthodox venue was, as Mrs Golding later admitted, that it was the only room they could get for nothing. At this meeting the women assembled decided to set up their own club, with no official reference to Rotary. Its initial objects were to foster friendship among the wives of Rotarians, and to organise as a club so that by co-operating and coordinating they could offer more in the way of service. As noted, they would be organisationally separate from Rotary, but would be ready to assist it when required. The club was limited to the wives or womenfolk of Manchester Rotarians or past Rotarians aged over 21. Meetings were to be held fortnightly on Tuesdays at 2.30 p.m. Subscription initially was £1 1s per annum. Those living too far from Manchester to be able to attend meetings regularly were admitted as associate members at a rate of 10s 6d. The first meeting of the newly constituted club took place on 10 January 1924, and it was at this time that a name was chosen for the club, referring to their position within the Rotarian emblem: The Inner Wheel; 10 January is still celebrated as 'Inner Wheel Day'.

At first this was a purely Manchester venture, but the name was soon taken up by other clubs, and in 1928 there was a joint meeting of the Manchester and Liverpool Inner Wheels, which was an area organisation according to Rotary Districts. It rapidly spread to other districts, and was so successful that from 1930 onwards facilities were provided at the RIBI annual conference for what was first called 'The Inner Wheel Business Meeting', effectively the annual general meeting. Additionally, a page of the RIBI organ *The Rotary Wheel* was henceforward devoted to Inner Wheel news. Finally, it was from this time that organisations of Rotary members' wives and female relatives were generally called Inner Wheel clubs, and were organised nationally; in 1934, the Association of Inner Wheel Clubs of Great Britain and Ireland was formally established. Later the Association developed its own emblem, of a wheel within a Rotary-style wheel, which can be worn as a lapel badge or brooch. Since 1977 the Association's headquarters have been located at 51 Warwick Square, London SW1.

The unofficial, albeit widely used, motto of the Inner Wheel is 'Friendship and Service', and friendship plays a major part in the clubs. This needs particular emphasis and work, because, unlike any of the other clubs dealt with in this book, the Inner Wheel has in the past had no control over admission of members. Although great care is taken in the selection of Rotarians, the Inner Wheel had no such check on admission. It had to accept their womenfolk, as they are called, whether they were peaceable or aggressive, sociable or anti-social, prim or earthy. There was for a long time no provision for requiring members to resign if their conduct or attitudes offended other members, and in the past there had even been resistance to suspending members for non-payment of subscription, although nowadays that is possibly the only reason for exclusion that is completely unambiguous. In practice, however, Inner Wheel members seem to behave as well, and to get on with each other at least as amicably, as members of other clubs where there is more opportunity for selection. There were originally three grades of membership: Active, Associate and Honorary. In fact the overwhelming majority of members have always fallen into the Active category, the Associate grade being used mainly for those women whose family relationship to Rotarians is tenuous. Active membership is open not only to wives of Rotarians, but their widows, widowed mothers, and widowed or unmarried sisters of unmarried Rotarians, over the age of eighteen, and living in a Rotarian's household. In practice, the distinction between grades of membership has become virtually meaningless, as qualifications for joining Inner Wheel clubs have been relaxed.

At a national level, Inner Wheel is financed by a levy raised on individual clubs at District level. Still, compared to Rotary, Inner Wheel is not at all a wealthy body. The main event of the Inner Wheel year is the annual conference, formerly known as the Rally, which since 1950 has taken place at the same venue as the RIBI conference, and which includes speakers and entertainment as well as the business meeting. One problem that has sometimes arisen is that while Rotary membership is based on the place of work, Inner Wheel members tend to be housewives, and hence are based at home, which may be some distance away, especially in major cities. Originally this led to Inner Wheel Districts being independent of Rotary Districts, but since the 1970s they have followed Rotary in this respect. There was at this time a tendency for growing Districts to divide and subdivide, which led to some dissatisfaction as friends found themselves separated.

This was distressing because of course friendship has always been heavily emphasised, and has been promoted through a range of social activities: for example, whist drives, social evenings, coffee mornings (for some reason known as American Teas), Christmas parties, ballroom dancing, outings to shows, garden parties, amateur dramatics and even, in a few clubs, choirs. Joint events with Rotary have also often been arranged. On a more educational level, many clubs have had an impressive programme of talks on a whole gamut of subjects from flower arranging through travel talks to world poverty and debt relief. Such activities are sometimes circumscribed by the increasing difficulty of finding affordable venues, although local authorities are often helpful in providing rooms in libraries or community centres. In this respect, it may well help that many Rotary husbands have prominent positions as officers in local authorities.

But it is by no means all social fun. Inner Wheel clubs have always been involved in service; at the first Inner Wheel meeting it was announced that a parcel of 80 woollen garments for babies had been sent to St Mary's Hospital in Manchester in time for Christmas. Fundraising activities are widespread, and have included bring and buy sales, jumble sales, raffles, and the like. Early on, 'baby bundles' along the lines mentioned above were organised to relieve child poverty, and poor mothers and children were sent on holiday. In the 1930s, Inner Wheel support for the Boots for Bairns campaign was strong. During the Second World War, many Inner Wheel clubs worked closely with the local Women's Voluntary Service, conducted savings campaigns and even made camouflage netting. Hospitality has always been a major feature of Inner Wheel activity; especially in wartime they entertained evacuees as well as service men and women. Since then, Inner Wheel women have regularly provided hospitality to visitors from overseas, and have assisted Rotary projects in many ways, so much so indeed that there seems in the past to have been a tendency for some Rotary Clubs to try to offload the drudgery of Rotary's community service on to the local Inner Wheel. This has been strongly resisted by Inner Wheel members, who do not see themselves as charwomen for Rotary. Their perspective was expressed by Millicent Gaskell in 1953: 'Always be ready to help, but never interfere'. Even so, the Inner Wheel has always acted to support Rotary projects. To quote Millicent Gaskell again, 'A good Inner Wheel wife makes a good Rotarian husband'. However, it is also very active on its own behalf. To take some examples of its contributions, in 1984 and in 2000 it presented to the Royal National Lifeboat Institute two fully equipped lifeboats, named appropriately *Inner Wheel* and *Inner Wheel II*; and it contributes regularly to cancer charities, children's hospices, riding for the disabled and the like. However, local Inner Wheels regularly take on local activities, such as providing lifts for the housebound, helping with shopping or housework and similar small but important activities.

Like Rotary, Inner Wheel is particularly active in international aid, unsurprisingly so, since it has long been an international organisation. In the 1930s, Inner Wheel clubs were formed in Australia, New Zealand and South Africa; in 1935 it also spread to Bergen, Norway, and after the Second World War throughout Europe and the rest of the world. In 1967 an umbrella organisation, International Inner Wheel, was finally formed, representing clubs in over 80 countries. In 2003 British Inner Wheel's *Magazine* claimed a circulation of 27,000.

Despite the fact that even well before this the Inner Wheel had become as international an organisation as Rotary, and despite its strong support for Rotary activity, it has not always met with the approval of Rotary International, as distinct from RIBI, which has in general been supportive. As already noted, from its outset Rotary had an emphatically masculine culture, and Rotary International traditionally looked askance at any involvement by women, despite founder Paul Harris's support for Inner Wheel style organisations. In 1951, Rotary International decided to crack down hard, and issued a directive stating that Rotary Clubs which gave recognition to any organisation of women which might or might not be using the word 'Rotary' in their names were:

> ... not acting within the framework of the constitutional documents of Rotary International and that such recognition should therefore be discontinued.

And so appeared to be calling for RIBI to dissociate itself completely from the Inner Wheel. RIBI managed to fend off this move, but was compelled to remove the Inner Wheel page from the Rotary magazine. This was not as severe a blow as it might have been, since wartime paper shortages had compelled the reduction of space available for Inner Wheel news in that magazine, and in 1942 the Cheltenham Inner Wheel had started producing its own *Newsletter*, which rapidly became that of the national Association. In 1951 this simply became the principal organ for Inner Wheel news, and it has continued to be so since, though now it is a smart publication called the *Inner Wheel Magazine*.

In 1962 Rotary International once again raised the issue, but by now Inner Wheel was ready with a tart statement to the effect that it was an autonomous organisation with its own constitution and funds, with the implication that since it did not interfere in Rotary International's affairs, RI should reciprocate. In this it appears to have had the full backing of RIBI. In any case, Rotary International gradually yielded to pressure, and at the 1982 Rotary International Convention in Dallas women's Rotary work was gratefully acknowledged, and Inner Wheel in particular was recognised. And as already indicated, in 1987, following on a Supreme Court ruling in the USA, restrictions on women imposed by Rotary were lifted, although it was still up to individual clubs whether they admitted women or not. A real turning point in Britain came in 1996, when the London Rotary Club finally succumbed and voted to raise its ban on women's membership, and in principle at least British women can become Rotarians. This has important implications for Inner Wheel, since many potential members can now bypass them and go straight to Rotary; also, there could possibly be demands for men to join Inner Wheel, although so far there seems to be no sign of this. In fact, fears about the bypassing of Inner Wheel have not been realised; only about 2 per cent of British Rotarians are women, and in any case Inner Wheel appeals to a different constituency.

One reason why women are not queuing up to join Rotary Clubs may be a continuing male culture in business, hence in Rotary. Those women who are involved in business or the professions are increasingly reluctant to go along with the attitudes implicit in this culture, and in any case, if they are interested in organisations that promote community service, there is a well-established one already in existence which is designed purely for women, namely Soroptimist International.

Soroptimist International

The Soroptimist movement in Britain originally arose as a reaction against Rotarian and other masculinism among women who saw similar opportunities for service, but had no connection with Rotary men, or even if they did, were unwilling to accept the subordinate position implied by the structure of the Inner Wheel. This was a time when women in business and the professions had become, through the influence of the women's suffrage movement and the effort put into war work by women, increasingly unwilling to return to the role of biddable helpmeet and hand back the serious work to men. It is therefore ironic that it owes its origin to a man. 'Soroptimism' (Latin 'soror' = sister plus 'optima' = best, or 'optimism') was first started in the USA by Stuart Morrow in 1921, and was built on the principle of a local grouping of the most outstanding women in each business and profession in a given district, along the lines of the Rotary Clubs. As noted above, at this time in various parts of Britain Rotary-style women's clubs were being formed, and became known as Venture Clubs, and there had been agitation for women's Rotary membership.

It was interesting that at the same time as this development was taking place, Stuart Morrow, apparently oblivious to it, was helping Lady Falmouth establish Britain's first Soroptimist Club, the London Club, which was started in 1923 and received its charter on St Valentine's Day, 1924. Stuart Morrow not only presented the Club with its charter, but installed its officers. Founding members included a theatre manager, a gynaecologist, an engineer and George Bernard Shaw's secretary; the actress Sybil Thorndike was also an early member, though possibly not a founder. Other early members included such noted suffragettes as Flora Drummond, and Mary Allen, later Commandant of the Women's Police Service. Finally there was an optician called Elizabeth Hawes who later became a major figure in Soroptimism. By 1927 Soroptimist Clubs had been established in Manchester, Liverpool, Glasgow and Edinburgh, and in 1930 the Soroptimists united with a number of other clubs that shared the same aims and objectives, principally the Venture Clubs of Great Britain, from which time they have all been known as Soroptimists. Initially, Soroptimist Clubs consisted of one member from each business or profession who was over 25 years of age and of high standing in her field of work. Like Rotary, the Soroptimists soon became organised into Federations. At first there were just two, namely the Americas, and Europe including Britain, but soon this was changed, and a Federation of Great Britain and Ireland was separated from that of Europe, making three federations; the Great Britain and Ireland Federation included members of the British Commonwealth, such as Australia, New Zealand and Canada. This situation continued until 1971, when Australia, New Zealand and Fiji formed the South-West Pacific Federation, though as will be noted later, many other Commonwealth countries are still included in the Great Britain and Ireland Federation.

The original Soroptimist International constitution, drafted by Eloise Cushing, a Californian lawyer, was:

> To foster the spirit of service as the basis of all worthy enterprises and to increase the efficiency of its members in the pursuit of their occupations by broadening their interest in the social, business and civic affairs of the community through an association of women representing diverse occupations.

Notice that there is no reference to the profit motive, or mutual business help, possibly because many of the original Soroptimists came not from business, but from service backgrounds; Stuart Morrow's inspiration originally came from discovering that a woman was the principal of a secretarial college. So it is unsurprising that the constitution's high-mindedness is reminiscent of the aims of the American General Federation of Women's Clubs referred to in Chapter 4, which already had half a century's experience of practising a service ethic. What is more interesting is the way in which it has transplanted successfully not only to Britain and Commonwealth countries, but to France: Suzanne Noel established the first French Soroptimist Club in Paris in 1924 at about the same time as Soroptimism was making its first mark in Britain. This was particularly remarkable in that, as has already been mentioned, in France the very idea of a women's club was considered bizarre. As Suzanne Noel put it,

> In 1924 women had no political rights, no personal freedom, and those demanding these rights were the subject of ridicule ... The word 'Soroptimist' is from a dubious Latin, something which did not make my job easier. In addition I was a specialist in plastic and cosmetic surgery unknown until then, and so it was said of me that I was a fool twice over.

Such folly did not, however, prevent her from promoting, or at least inspiring, Soroptimist Clubs in many countries of Europe and beyond, notably the Netherlands, Italy, Austria (the Vienna Club was particularly prominent), Hungary and Estonia, as well as Japan.

The classification of members of the French Soroptimist Clubs was rather different from the Anglo-American norm, having more representatives of the arts than usual elsewhere, but in other ways it closely resembled them. From the outset the Soroptimists' purpose has been to advance the status of women, maintain high ethical standards in business and professional life, and develop unity amongst Soroptimists in all countries. This is reflected in the Soroptimist emblem, designed by Anita Houts Thompson, and adopted in 1928, sometimes referred to irreverently as 'Soroptimist Sally'. It 'represents womanhood with her arms uplifted in a gesture of freedom and acceptance of the responsibilities of the best and highest good'. This acceptance leads them to various sorts of activity. In the 1930s, especially in Europe, they were often concerned with protecting the rights of professional and businesswomen from economic discrimination, and resisting the governmental exclusion of women by Fascist régimes. Additionally, during the Second World War, Soroptimist Clubs in occupied countries engaged in covert aid activities otherwise atypical of Soroptimism, such as gathering in a member's home before curfew and spending the night making and mending clothes for deprived civilians. In Britain before the war Soroptimist Clubs were much involved in aid work to refugees, and in securing the escape of fellow Soroptimists, especially by sponsoring members of the Vienna Club after the 1938 *Anschluss* with Germany. During the war, British Soroptimists contributed in various ways, most visibly when the then President of the British and Irish Federation, Alice Williams, presented three ambulances, one Canadian and two British, all bearing the Soroptimist emblem, to the British Army on Horse Guards Parade, London. Less spectacularly, members regularly did the sort of work associated with the Women's Voluntary Service, such as staffing canteens. Clubs also established rest rooms for women in the forces and organised flag days to raise funds for those made homeless by air raids.

As indicated above, European Soroptimists had had a particularly hard time of it during the war, and when the British Soroptimist Federation held its conference in London in 1945, just three representatives of European clubs, including Suzanne Noel, were able to attend. However, the post-war period saw not only a rapid revival of Soroptimist Clubs but a vigorous expansion; by 1960 Soroptimism counted 1,342 clubs in 31 countries, with an overall membership of 40,622, and in 1973 the name 'Soroptimist International' became the movement's official title. Since 1945 the movement has worked closely with the United Nations and its agencies. Like Rotary and Inner Wheel, Soroptimist International's main service concerns at present are with international aid and development. Although previously much general work had been done, especially in connection with refugees, it was in the 1970s that funds began to be raised for specific projects, first with a concerted effort to provide a fleet of motorised boats to aid health care in the archipelago of the Maldives, and rapidly expanded. The organisation is in general concerned with issues such as human rights, the environment, health, the status of women, economic and social development and the fostering of international goodwill and understanding.

As already noted, the division by federation can make titles a little misleading; for example, for historical reasons Soroptimist International of Great Britain and Ireland has 12,000 members not only in the nations of Britain and Ireland, but in Anguilla, Antigua and Barbuda, Bangladesh , Barbados, British Virgin Islands, Cameroon, The Gambia, Grenada, India, Jamaica, Malawi, Malta, Mauritius, Mozambique, Nigeria, Pakistan, Seychelles, Sierra Leone, South Africa, Sri Lanka, St Vincent and the Grenadines, Trinidad and Tobago, Turks and Caicos, Uganda, and Zimbabwe. Like Inner Wheel it has its annual general meetings at a different location each year; unlike Inner Wheel, it can decide its own time and venue independently of any other organisation. The Federation's publication is *Soroptimist News*, issued six times a year; *The International Soroptimist*, covering all Federations, is quarterly. Its specifically service-oriented activities have included such local initiatives as providing housing for retired business or professional women; participating in the work of youth clubs, particularly with handicapped children; helping out such groups as Contact the Elderly; fundraising for charities; and of course co-operating with other women's organisations at a local level. However, it is also very visible at national and international level. In 2005, for instance, among other concerns, it participated in Home Office initiatives to review the law on prostitution; it campaigned on domestic violence; through SI's 'Project Independence: Women Survivors of War', it worked hard to support women by providing them with the skills they need to rebuild their lives after war; and more generally it has supported campaigns to improve the environment.

All this makes the Soroptimists seem like a very high-minded serious set of women. Indeed they are; but they are much more besides. At the 2005 annual general meeting at Bournemouth, in order to raise funds for the above-mentioned Project Independence, the Project Liaison officer took bets from Soroptimists willing to dye her hair green; she raised £250 in one evening, enough to pay for one woman's training. Also in aid of Project Independence, in 2004 a London Soroptimist with the stage name CasSandra sang jazz at a high-profile fundraising dinner at the Langham Hotel. At local level, fundraising is supported and accompanied by a whole range of social activities such as outings and visits, for example to Burnham Beeches Forest or to the Lord Chancellor's residence; talks on a variety of topics; entertainments, as when the St Albans and District Club in 2003 hosted *An Evening with Noel Coward*, and in 2004 organised a theatre outing to see Edward Taylor's play *Murder by Misadventure*; and of course a range of more traditional fundraisers, like cheese and wine parties, barbecues, garden parties, bridge drives and sponsored walks. Friendship and a lively social participation in the cause of service is at least as important to 'Sorops' as it is to Inner Wheel women.

Despite all this activity, Soroptimists complain that the profile of the organisation in the UK is very low and that, in the words of Soroptimist Peggy Simpson, Soroptimists are the world's best-kept secret. In many other countries, such as Australia, the USA and many developing countries, SI seems to be more highly regarded, which means the organisation can be more effective. One of the problems in Britain is competition. As one London Soroptimist puts it,

> In London anyway, I would say the environment has reached saturation point with world orientated organisations and individuals so that nothing stands out unless you put a lot of time, effort and money behind it, and we don't have any of those requirements to spare.

This comes down to the usual problems with women's activity; women have so many demands made on their time and energy that they have little left to spare for voluntary service. Also, despite the advances of women over the years, business especially is still very much a male-dominated world, operating in a male culture.

Business and professional women are likely to suffer from a glass ceiling that prevents them from using top job power and influence to further women's causes, though it should be said that Rotarians are not always quite as highly placed as is often assumed. As RIBI General Secretary David Morehen admitted in *The Times* of 26 April 1996, 'Our average member is ... probably No. 2 at his trade, because No. 1 is too busy'. But of course a big difference between Soroptimists and Rotarians is that Soroptimists do not have wives, and cannot rely on the automatic assumption of support from 'womenfolk'. Women competing with men particularly in business have long had cause to complain that as well as doing their job they have to cope with all the domestic details that businessmen traditionally have left to their wives. On the other hand, as a women-only organisation unconnected to any other, Soroptimists do not have to deal with other traditional male assumptions. For example, as mentioned above, there has sometimes been a perception that some Rotarians have regarded Inner Wheel as a means of shuffling off the drudgery of service work onto the people who traditionally have to deal with drudgery, namely women. This is obviously an attitude that Inner Wheel is not happy with, and that SI does not have to contend with.

Even so, Inner Wheel is of course intimately related to Rotary, while Soroptimist International has from the outset been fiercely independent, and has little in common with Rotary or Inner Wheel except the service ethic. However, that is a big exception. In practice, both Inner Wheel and Soroptimist International do co-operate with each other on various projects. They represent another example of women claiming a space initially occupied by men, and in their differing ways emphasising their independent and highly practical commitment to the ideals of service proclaimed by men.

Major sources for this chapter

Roger Levy's *Rotary International* is an excellent history by an insider of long standing, and Millicent Gaskell, another high-profile insider, wrote *Home and Horizon* about the Inner Wheel. For more recent information, see Jay French and Kathleen Hovey on the Inner Wheel, and Janet Haywood on Soroptimist International. Also worth browsing are the periodicals: the *Rotarian*, *Soroptimist News* and *International Soroptimist*, and the *Inner Wheel Association Magazine*. The authors are especially indebted to Irene Cockcroft for information on Soroptimist International.

9   And what now?

'Kids today just aren't joiners.'
(Putnam 2000)

This overview so far has concentrated on people who would be regarded as joiners, going back well over two centuries. However, over the past generation a problem has been identified by various people, but most blatantly Robert Putnam in his oft-cited *Bowling Alone*, published in 2000. People just aren't joining any more.

For those who have not read *Bowling Alone*, the title may need some explanation. It had come to Putnam's attention that patterns of participation in ten-pin bowling, one of the traditional occupations of the red-blooded American male, had changed considerably in the late twentieth century. Whereas even in the 1970s men joined teams to compete with other teams in bowling leagues, by the 1990s the more usual pattern was for men to go to bowling alleys and play alone. This led Putnam to look at other forms of social interaction, or joining.

It has frequently been remarked in recent years that people who sign up to clubs and voluntary associations of the traditional sort tend to be well over forty, and then find that they are the babies of the group, whose average age may be seventy. Putnam cites various possible causes for this, based admittedly on North American experience, and why this worries him. First of all he raises the concept of 'social capital', while admitting that this is at least the fifth time this term has been invented independently in the twentieth century, including by the sociologist Pierre Bourdieu in the 1950s. As used by Putnam, 'social capital' seems to be another name for what has especially since the fall of the Soviet Empire been referred to by such diverse authorities as Jürgen Habermas and the supporters of Pope John Paul II as 'civil society'. It has to be said that a concern for this perception of 'civil society' is relatively recent. In the earlier twentieth century, as obliquely mentioned earlier, the concept of 'joiners' was not necessarily regarded in a positive light, by the British and American intelligentsia in particular. Sinclair Lewis has already been quoted in connection with his disdain for Rotarians, Kiwanis, Oddfellows, Masons and similar groups. Similarly in Britain 'Bloomsbury' tended to be rather loftily amused about the idea of all these middle- and lower-class people joining organisations, although, as mentioned in earlier chapters, Virginia Woolf before the First World War had not only signed up to the People's Suffrage Federation and as a volunteer was licking envelopes for them, but by 1932 she had even become an active member of the London and National Society for Women's Service. Later, she was also elected Treasurer of the Rodmell Women's Institute in rural Sussex. But most 'Bloomsberries' remained aloof.

However, a disdainful or suspicious attitude towards 'joining' was not typical of the population as a whole. As we have shown, from the mid-nineteenth century for over a hundred years women and working class men were happy to form their own clubs and associations. Clubbability may not have been approved of by the more rarefied intelligentsia, but at least up to the 1950s in Britain the majority of people of all classes seem to have had no problem with joining up to a wide and varied range of organistions. These included those we have dealt with, such as clubs, institutes, guilds, Scouts, Guides and the like, but also those we have passed over as not being sufficiently contested from the point of view of gender, such as amateur choirs. The early twentieth century in Britain was probably the country's high point for 'joining', or at least for communal activities. As well as the mass gymnastics which the Women's League of Health and Beauty among others practised, there was the phenomenon of community singing, as mocked in *Brave New World* by Aldous Huxley, who was of course a Bloomsberry. Again, as already noted, collective youth activities flourished: Scouts, Guides, Boys' and Girls' Brigades, Kibbo Kift, Woodland Folk and the like have been referred to in Chapter 6. But by the end of the twentieth century, this had all changed. Instead of mass gymnastic displays, people went singly to gyms to work out on their own fitness programmes, usually plugged into their own Walkmans or iPods, so as to cut out any possibility of social interaction. Masses of people go to Woodstock or Glastonbury, but not to participate in communal music: their role at least as regards music is as a passive audience. In Britain at least in the early twenty-first century, billboard and flyposted advertisements for 'gentleman's clubs' conjure up images not of leather armchairs and crusted port but of lap dancing (at minimum) and Bacardi Breezers. And of course for young women the stereotypical image of 'going clubbing' tends to mean dancing solo round a handbag, in the sort of lighting disastrous to anybody with epileptic tendencies, accompanied by music played at an amplification that precludes any sort of conversation below the level of shouting. And to cap it all, most of our preceding chapters have ended on a note of decline, if not exactly fall. Change certainly, and possibly decay.

So what happened over that half-century from 1950 to 2000? One factor in the increasing dislike of collective activities is their association with totalitarian régimes both of the right and especially the left. For instance, British television watchers of a certain age will remember the radical director John Grierson being reduced by 1960 to presenting clips of gymnastic displays from Eastern Europe, the Soviet Union, China and North Korea, which was enough to put anybody off even synchronised swimming. Putnam, however, relying on North American experience, where this played much less of a part, looks for other factors. Feminist hackles may be raised briefly by his identification of part of the problem with women taking up full-time jobs, and having less time for volunteering or general social get-togethers, although the problem of the full-time working mother is also known in Europe. Putnam also cites pressures of time and money, shopping mall culture, and mobility and sprawl, quoting one Southern Californian woman who remarks, 'I live in Garden Grove, shop in Santa Ana, go to the dentist in Anaheim, my husband works in Long Beach, and I used to be President of the League of Women Voters in Fullerton'. This also implies the time spent in sheer travelling between home and work, which in major cities usually takes up a good two hours or more a day. There is also the matter of television ('TV watching and volunteering don't go together'), to say nothing of what Putnam calls 'cyberbalkanisation':

> the internet enables us to confine our communications to people who share precisely our interest – not just other BMW owners, but owners of BMW 2002s, and perhaps even owners of turbocharged 1973 2002s, regardless of where they live and what other interests they and we have.

Thus it might seem that as such free associations as clubs began in the Enlightenment as expressions of individual freedom from Church and State, this stage of society has passed. The modern global world, having rejected not only Church and State, but any forms of collective interaction, is now suffering from an atomised individualism that precludes any but the most nerdish social interaction. It may well be that 'civil society' is as much a temporary phenomenon as 'feudal society'; even if there ever was such a thing as 'feudalism', which most medieval historians dispute, it has long since ceased to exist except as a term of political abuse. According to this view, the same fate may be in store for the equally imprecisely-defined 'civil societies', and because clubs and associations are seen as an important part of that, they are also doomed. We are increasingly locked into our own individual modules, with nothing but the minimum of social interaction. Fragmentation rules OK. The world of *The Matrix* is upon us.

Well, up to a point. Even Putnam cites examples to suggest that we may be experiencing less of a decline in social interaction than a change in its modes. To take one instance: as regards 'cyberbalkanisation', it is not only nerds who visit chat rooms, and, despite what the popular press claims, by no means all those who participate in them are seeking to exploit vulnerable young girls. Chat rooms, email lists and the like, as well as having a distinct downside, can also fulfil the sort of role performed in early modern society by the type of correspondence that led to the formation of the Royal Society, among other phenomena, by allowing free discussion among people often separated by thousands of miles, much of which is mere fannishness, but at least some of which is severely academic. For example, anybody interested in medieval European literature or indeed post-Roman British history should certainly visit the archives of the Arthurnet email list to be assured that there is a forbiddingly high level of scholarship on display; and those who subscribe to other extremely varied lists, such as those concerned with women's history or the history of sexuality, will spring forward in defence of the very learned correspondence that emerges from forums where ideas can be floated without having to be submitted to a journal editor for peer review and assessment of whether such ideas meet with the automatic acceptance of the scholarly community. And even quitting cyberspace, Putnam refers to the growth in encounter groups, reading circles, support groups, and such self-help groups as Alcoholics Anonymous. Reading groups are a particularly significant phenomenon; in the USA, this has particularly resulted in the transformation of women's reading groups into first a civic movement and then a political force. Also in Britain women's clubs, although much reduced in number, still manage to keep going. In London alone, since at least 1990 the imminent demise of the University Women's Club has been predicted, but at the time of writing in 2005 it is still managing successfully to provide services for such women as can afford it; again, the Sloane Club is a transformation of military women's clubs into something rather wider, which appears at least to be surviving, or even flourishing; and for the very well-to-do woman, the Lansdowne Club provides unrivalled facilities. These are just a few examples; there are many others both for the wealthy and the less so. Associations like the WI and the Soroptimists show little sign of decline, to mention but two.

Are joiners dying out?

One factor that is frequently cited in descrptions of an increasingly unclubbable society is the rising age-profile in clubs and associations. To some extent at least, this may be a function of changing work patterns. In the past, many clubs and associations were kept going by women who did not go to work, either because their husbands earned enough to maintain the household, or because they had independent means. Even those who went to work in white-collar occupations usually had enough time to take part in non-work- and non-home-related activities. Nowadays, as already indicated, a work culture of long hours, or shorter hours combined with home and family responsibilities, together with increasing commuting time, often means that the only other activity a woman of working age feels like undertaking is collapsing in front of the TV. And as for those of independent means, the classic *rentier* living comfortably on the income from invested capital is almost a vanished breed. So when the older generation who are still joiners are no longer with us, there will be no more of this sort of social interaction.

However, there is now a new class of person of independent means: the retired, especially those on occupational pensions with benefit defined from final salary, who not only tend to live longer and remain physically and mentally active longer than they did a couple of generations ago, but, having disposed of expenditure on child care, education and mortgage, are relatively well-to-do. These are now the people who have the time, energy and income to run voluntary associations, and it is particularly noticeable that not only are the people running the show the vigorous elderly, but the majority of them are women. Demographics, together with the growing reluctance of employers to contribute to pension funds and the growing tendency of governments to regard them as milch-cows, probably means that this too is a temporary phenomenon, but at least for the next generation in Britain it is definitely here.

What happens when the present generation of comfortable pensioners confronts mortality? It may be apposite to refer to the experience of a Western journalist in the Soviet Union in the 1960s, when religion of any sort was strongly discouraged. On visiting an Eastern Orthodox church, the journalist noticed that most of the congregation consisted of old women, and asked a young priest, 'What will you do when all the grandmothers die?' The priest replied serenely, 'God will make more grandmothers'. Without wishing to push the analogy, and, noting that despite appearances at the time, those who knew Russia could attest that the Church could call on a more covert congregation of much younger people who were finally mobilised in the 1980s, we should note that at the time of writing the Orthodox Church in Russia is not only highly popular but is effectively an arm of the State, which ironically is now a matter of concern, not least for feminists. Whether clubs and associations in Britain will similarly revive is a matter of speculation only. We can only note that over the past two centuries they have provided women not only with spaces of their own but a series of arenas in which to contest their exclusion. At present it is older women by and large who are maintaining that tradition.

Women in the late twentieth and early twenty-first centuries

Leaving aside generalities about social capital, civil society and social interaction, it cannot be denied that in the last half of the twentieth century the social standing of women in Europe and North America has improved enormously. In the Introduction, we cited the case of British nurses coming off late shift to find themselves refused service in hamburger restaurants in the 1960s; and we repeat that in the early 1970s it was by no means unknown for single women in professional posts that assured a substantial salary, who were able to provide a more than adequate deposit, to be told that they could not be granted a mortgage to buy an apartment unless they could find a man willing to sign up as surety for them (this at a time when building societies were blithely offering men mortgages at rates that they could not then hope to repay). Nowadays that would be unthinkable. In Europe and North America legislation and custom have combined to make it so. In Britain since 1975, the Equal Opportunities Commission has kept a watchful eye on discrimination against women in all areas of public life. Women on their own can no longer be barred from pubs. Only a few West End gentlemen's clubs still hold out against women. Women's soccer is becoming widely popular to the extent, as already noted, that it can be shown live by the BBC on a non-digital channel. Even at Wimbledon, the All-England Lawn Tennis and Croquet Club has finally conceded women's right to be given equal competition status. Barriers to women's employment are gradually being lowered. The wife of the current Prime Minister of the United Kingdom is a top lawyer practising under her maiden name of Cherie Booth and specialising in the field of human rights. We are, it appears, moving ever closer to a situation of social equality, where the need for separate women's clubs and indeed other women-only organisations can be dispensed with. Yet this view also falls far short of the whole picture.

It is frequently pointed out that despite all sorts of legislation, women's average pay is at best three-quarters of men's. *The Economist* (4 June 2005) in citing the term 'glass ceiling' has suggested that 'glass partition' might be more appropriate. For example, repeating earlier Soviet experience, British women are increasingly entering the medical profession, but because largely of family commitments are more likely to be part-time workers, have lengthy career breaks, or both. Thus they can find themselves stranded in comparatively lowly and less well-paid posts unless they are already wealthy enough to be able to unload household chores onto paid staff. Similar tendencies are observable in other professions, particularly the law. Another more ominous factor retarding women's progress towards meaningful equality is violence. Domestic violence against women shows no sign of a downturn, and the difficulty that many police forces and courts appear to have in dealing with cases of rape continues to cause alarm. So women still have some way to go in most social areas to reach the stage when they need no longer fear men's competition or violence. Why this should be so is somewhat puzzling. It is interesting that in the 1970s and 1980s in Britain a wide variety of women found a social as well as a political outlet in the feminist movement, campaigning on the issues we have mentioned, and some campaigns, especially those connected with the proposed deployment of nuclear missiles at the US Air Force base at Greenham Common in the 1980s, attracted mass support from many unlikely sectors of female society. Women from mining communities campaigning against pit closures had a similar if more restricted impact. And yet, despite T-shirts proclaiming 'I'll be a post-feminist in post-patriarchy', by the mid-1990s the feminist movement in Britain was at best struggling, and in the early twenty-first century it is little more than a memory. Feminist historians point out that this has happened before; in 1935 such different women as the former suffragist Ray Strachey and the hard-line Christian Dorothy L. Sayers were bemoaning the lack of feminist consciousness among young women, and even in 1952 Marghanita Laski, of all people, saw the feminist movement as a laudable venture in history which had triumphantly achieved its aims but which had nothing to do with her ordinary life in the present. Fifteen years later she had changed her mind, helping to prove Dale Spender's frequently uttered dictum in the 1980s to the effect that every fifty years women have to re-invent the wheel. Depressingly, for many women feminism remains an f-word, despite the fact that women's equality still has a fair way to go, and the opposition to it is not only getting more vociferous but more physically violent.

Therefore it is evident that there still appears to be a real need for women to claim their own space, as is recognised for example by the University Women's

Club. This is one of the reasons why in Britain various attempts to bring 'private clubs' into the remit of the 1975 Sex Discrimination Act have so far failed. This is not to say that there have not been strenuous efforts made to achieve this. One such went to the House of Lords in 2002, with no satisfactory conclusion. Another was debated in the Commons in 2004, but fell by the wayside basically because it was inquorate. So for the time being at least single-sex clubs continue to operate, even if they do not always flourish. Women still to a considerable extent have to assert their right to leisure time. There are still considerable pressures to make women feel guilty if they take time off. Regular TV-watching couch potatoes may note that Homer Simpson may happily slump in front of the television before heading off to Moe's Bar, but Marge still has to clear up after him.

And yet, as noted above, by no means all is gloom and doom. It has frequently if surreptitiously been stated that measures for the improvement of women's social and economic status have not always been dependent on a vigorous feminist movement. The presence of a number of vehement women in Parliament, and some only marginally less so in government, indicates that women's issues are not going to be totally sidelined, at least in the near future. And on a less exalted level, the presence of women in various organisations which are not traditional clubs is diminished by very little if at all. To return to the Women's Institutes, the membership recorded by their National Federation has indeed fallen over recent decades, from a quarter of a million to 220,000. This is still a membership figure that political parties of any colour would sell their policies for. In context, the apparent decline of women's social activity still makes women's groups, if not traditional clubs, seem like a factor that politicians could spend more time studying.

Thus it appears that although the clubs and associations we have covered in the foregoing chapters may be declining, or even in a number of cases already extinct, this does not mean that women no longer come together for social purposes. They definitely do, but not always in traditional ways, although many still are active in social organisations of the sort that are mentioned above. Women may no longer be clubbable in a way that would have been comprehensible and acceptable to élite males of the early twentieth century, but their participation in sporting activities, in politics and indeed in the WI, TG or Soroptimists, shows that a significant number of women have succumbed neither to television, cyberbalkanisation nor domesticity. Long may this continue to be the case.

Bibliography

Andrews, Donna T. 'Popular Culture and Public Debate: London 1780' in: *The Historical Journal* v. 39 (1996)

Andrews, Maggie *The Acceptable Face of Feminism* London: Lawrence and Wishart, 1997

Anstruther, Eva 'Ladies' Clubs' in: *Nineteenth Century* v. 45 (April 1899)

Baden-Powell, Agnes *How Girls Can Help to Build Up the Empire: The Handbook for Girl Guides* London: Girl Guides Association, 1912

Baden-Powell, Robert *Aids to Scouting for NCOs and Men* London: Gale and Potter, 1899

Baden-Powell, Robert *Lessons from the Varsity of Life* London: C. Arthur Pearson, 1934

Baden-Powell, Robert *Rovering to Success* London: H. Jenkins, 1922

Baden-Powell, Robert *Scouting for Boys* London: C. Arthur Pearson, 1908

Badminton Magazine of Sports and Pastimes – Monthly. 1895–1914

Beetham, Margaret and Boardman, Kay *Victorian Women's Magazines* Manchester: Manchester University Press, 2001

Benson, E.F. *As We Are: A Modern Review* London: Longmans Green, 1932

Binns, Graham, Massingberd, Hugh and Markham, Sheila *A House of the First Class: the Travellers Club and its members* London: The Travellers Club, 2003

Bland, Lucy *Banishing the Beast* London: Penguin, 1995

Bush, Julia *Edwardian Ladies and Imperial Power* Leicester: Leicester University Press, 2000

Carrick, Neil and Ashton, Edward L. *The Athenaeum, Liverpool, 1797–1997* Liverpool: The Athenaeum, 1997

Catt, Frederick Charles *Report on The First Hundred Years of the Bengeo Working Men's Club, 1878–1978* Hertford: Bengeo Working Men's Club, 1978

Cawthorne, J. and Desira, C. *All About Us* London: GFS Platform, 2002

Cholmondley, Essex *The Story of Charlotte Mason* London: Dent, 1960

Clark, Peter *British Clubs and Societies 1580–1800: the origins of an associational world* (Oxford Studies in Social History) Oxford: Oxford University Press, 2000

Commission for Racial Equality *Mount Pleasant Working Men's Club: report of a formal investigation ...* London: The Commission, 1979

Commission for Racial Equality *The Woodhouse Recreation Club and Social Institute, Leeds: report of a formal investigation ...* London: The Commission, 1980

Coote, C.R. *The Other Club* London: Sidgwick and Jackson, 1971

Cossay, Rosalynda *Golfing Ladies* London: Orbis, 1984

Crawford, Elizabeth *The Women's Suffrage Movement: a reference guide 1866–1928* London: UCL Press, 1999

Crichton-Miller, H.C. 'The Adolescent Girl and the Guide Movement' in: *Girl Guides Annual Report, 1926*

Croly, Jennie Cunningham *The History of the Women's Club Movement in America* New York, NY: Henry G. Allen, 1898

Darwin, Bernard *British Clubs* London: Collins, 1943

Davies, Margaret Llewelyn *Life As We Have Known It* London: Women's Co-operative Guild, 1931

Davies, Margaret Llewelyn *Maternity: letters from working women* London: G. Bell, 1915

Davies, Margaret Llewelyn *The Women's Co-operative Guild 1883–1904* Kirby Lonsdale: The Guild, 1904

D'Espaigne, Dora 'The Lyceum Club for Ladies' in: *Lady's Realm* (1904)

Dibble, Jeremy C. Hubert H. Parry: his life and music Oxford: Oxford University Press, 1992

Dockrell, Emily Morgan 'Women's Clubs' in: *The Humanitarian* v. 12 (1898)

Dove, Iris *Sisterhood or Surveillance?* University of Greenwich PhD Thesis, 1996

Dunbar, J. *Peg Woffington and the World* London: Heinemann, 1968

Dyhouse, Carol *Girls Growing Up in Late Victorian and Edwardian England* London: Routledge, 1981

Englishwoman ed. Ella Hepworth Dixon – Monthly. London: 1895–9

Englishwoman's Review – Quarterly. London: 1866–1910

Escott, T.H.S. *Club Makers and Club Members* London: T. Fisher Unwin, 1914

Firebrace, Cordell W. *The Army and Navy Club, 1837–1933* London: Murray, 1934

First Aid Nursing Yeomanry Gazette, 1915–

Firth, A.H. *The Junior: A history of the Junior United Service Club, 1827–1929* London: Junior United Service Club, 1929

French, Jay *Inner Wheel: a history* London: Association of Inner Wheel Clubs, 1977

Friederichs, Hulda 'A Peep at the Pioneer Club' in: *Young Woman* v. 4 (1896)

Gaffin, Jean and Thoms, David *Caring and Sharing* Manchester: Co-operative Union, 1983

Galsworthy, John *On Forsyte Change* London: Heinemann, 1930

Galsworthy, John *The Man of Property* London: Heinemann, 1906

Gaskell, Millicent *Home and Horizon: an account of the history and organization of the Association of Inner Wheel Clubs* London: The Association, 1953

Gender and Sport: a reader ed. Sheila Scraton and Anne Flintoff, London: Routledge, 2002

Gibb, John 'Golf War' in: *The Spectator* 7 December 2002

Girls' Friendly Society *Annual Report 2001*

Girtin, Tom *The Abominable Clubman* London: Hutchinson, 1962

Graves, Charles *Leather Armchairs* London: Cassell, 1961

Griffiths, M. *Clubs and Clubmen* London: Hutchinson, 1907

Hargreaves, Jennifer *Sporting Females* London: Routledge, 1994

Harrison, Brian 'For Church, Queen and Family: the Girls' Friendly Society 1874–1920' in: *Past and Present* no. 61 (November 1973)

Haywood, Janet *The History of Soroptimist International* Cambridge: Soroptimist International, 1995

Heath-Stubbs, M. *Friendship's Highway* London: GFS, 1935

Holland, C. 'The Girl Guides: A National Training Organisation' in: *Girl Guides' Annual Report, 1923*

Hough, Richard *The Ace of Clubs: a history of the Garrick* London: Andre Deutsch, 1986

Housing Women: A Celebration of YWCA housing since 1855 London: YWCA, 2000

Hovey, Kathleen *Friendship Through Service: the story of Inner Wheel* London: Association of Inner Wheel Clubs of Great Britain and Ireland, 2004

Jackson, Louis C. *A History of the United Service Club* London: United Service Club, 1937

Jenkins, Inez *The History of the Women's Institute Movement of England and Wales* Oxford: National Federation of Women's Institutes, 1953

Jones, Dora M. 'The Ladies' clubs of London' in: *Young Woman* v. 7 (1899)

Joy, Nancy *Maiden Over* London: Sporting Handbooks, 1950

Kenealy, Arabella *Feminism and Sex-extinction* London: Fisher Unwin,1920

Kenealy, Arabella 'Woman as athlete' in: *Nineteenth Century* v. 45 (1899)

Kerr, Rose M. *The Story of the Girl Guides* London: Girl Guides Association, 1954

Kinnaird, Emily *Reminiscences* London: Murray, 1923

Knollys, Beatrice 'Ladies' Clubs in London' in: *The Englishwoman*' (May 1895)

'Ladies' Clubs' (anon.) in: *Tinsley's Magazine* v. 4 (1869)

The Lady: a journal for gentlewomen – Monthly. London: 1885–

Lees-Milne, James 'The Second World War' in: Ziegler, P. and Seward, D. (eds) *Brooks's* London: Constable, 1991

Lejeune, Anthony *The Gentlemen's Clubs of London* London: MacDonald and Jane's, 1979

The Letters of Dorothy L. Sayers ed. Barbara Reynolds (v. 2) Swavesey, Cambs.: The Dorothy L. Sayers Society, 1997

Levy, Roger *Rotary International in Great Britain and Northern Ireland* London: Macdonald and Evans, 1978

Linton, Elizabeth Lynn *The New Woman in Haste and at Leisure* New York: Merriam, 1895

Longrigg, Doreen *Ladies on the Fairway* Speldhurst: Midas Books, 1981

McCrone, Kathleen E. *Sport and the Physical Emancipation of Women 1870–1914* London: Routledge, 1988

Macfie, A.B.S. *The Curious History of Toc H Women's Association, 1917–1928* London: Toc H Women's Association, 1954

Macfie, A.B.S. *The Further History of Toc H Women's Association: onwards from 1928* London: Toc H Women's Association, 1960

Marwick, Arthur *Women at War, 1914–18* London: Fontana, 1977

Mayhew, Henry *Report Concerning the Trade and Hours of Closing Usual … Among the So-called 'Working Men's Clubs'* London: [s.n.], 1871

Merz, Caroline *After the Vote* London: National Union of Townswomen's Guilds, 1988

Molloy, J.F. *The Life and Adventures of Peg Woffington* (3rd ed.) London: Hurst and Blackett, 1887

Moor, Lucy M. *Girls of Yesterday and Today: The romance of the YWCA* London: S.W. Partridge, 1911

Morris, Jan *Conundrum* London: Faber and Faber, 1974

Murtagh, Niall *The Blue-eyed Salaryman* London: Profile, 2004

Nevill, Ralph *London Clubs: their history and their treasures* London: Chatto and Windus, 1911

Nicholson, Joyce *Why Women Lose at Bridge* London: Gollanz; Peter Crawley, 1985

Nulli Secundus Club: History and Notes and list of members London: Chiswick Press, 1922

O'Connor, Anthony *Clubland: the wrong side of the right people* London: Martin Brian and O'Keefe, 1975

Percival, Alice C. *Youth Will Lead* London: Collins, 1931

Pethick, Emmeline 'Working Girls' Clubs' in: Reason, W. (ed.) *University and Social Settlements* London: Methuen, 1898

Pethick-Lawrence, Frederick W. *Fate Has Been Kind* London: Hutchinson, 1943

Phelps, Barry *Power and the Party: a history of the Carlton Club 1882–1982* London: Macmillan, 1982

Pollard, Marjorie *Cricket for Women and Girls* London: Hutchinson, 1934

Popham, H. *FANY: the story of the Women's Transport Service* London: Leo Cooper/Secker and Warburg, 1984

Porter, Roy *London: a social history* Harmondsworth: Penguin, 2000

Putnam, Robert D. *Bowling Alone: the collapse and revival of American community* New York; London: Simon and Schuster, 2000

Rappaport, Erika D. *Shopping for Pleasure: women in the making of London's West End* Princeton: Princeton UP, 2000

Robertson, C. Grant 'Why I Believe in the Girl Guides' in *Girl Guides' Annual Report 1925*

Robertson, J.W. *The Story of the Women's Institute Movement in England and Wales* Idbury, Knigham, Oxon: The Village Press, 1925

Rogers, Barbara *Men Only* London: Pandora, 1988

Rooff, Madeline *Youth and Leisure: a survey of girls' organisations in England and Wales* Edinburgh: Constable, 1935 'Prepared ... under the auspices of the National Council of Girls' Clubs'

Rosanvallon, Pierre *Le modèle politique français* Paris: Editions du Seuil, 2003

Rubinstein, David *Before the Suffragettes* Hassocks: Harvester, 1986

Sadler, Michael 'Girl Guides and the Community' in: *Girl Guides Annual Report 1927*

Sampson, Antony *Anatomy of Britain* London: Hodder and Stougton, 1962

Shafts: for women and the working class ed. M. Shurmer Sibthorpe – Weekly/monthly, London: M. Shurmer Sibthorpe, 1892–9

Sharp, Evelyn *Buyers and Builders* London: Women's Co-operative Guild, 1933

Shipley, Stan *Club Life and Socialism in mid-Victorian London* London: Journeyman, 1983

Smedley, Constance *Crusaders* London: Duckworth, 1929

'Some Thoughts on our Early Years' in: *Association of Women's Solicitors* v. 8 (December 2002–February 2003)

Sparrow, Violet *The History of the Bishop's Stortford Working Men's Club* Bishop's Stortford: The Club, 1987

Stanley, Maude *Clubs for Working Girls* London: Macmillan, 1890

Stanley, Maude *Work about the Five Dials* London: Macmillan, 1878

Stott, Mary *Organisation Woman: the story of the Townswomen's Guilds* London: Heinemann, 1978

Taylor, John *From Self-help to Glamour: the working man's club, 1860–1972* (History Workshop Pamphlets: 7) Oxford: History Workshop, 1972

Thale, Mary 'Women in London debating societies in 1780' in: *Gender and History* v. 7 no. 1 (April 1995)

Thompson, Vronwyn M. *1910...And Then?* London: Girl Guides Association, 1990

Thornley, John *History of the Grand United Order of Oddfellows* Burton-on-Trent: [s.n.], 1913

Tibbs, J. *Club Life of London* London: Richard Bentley, 1866

Toc H Journal, London Toc H: 1922–67

Tranter, Neil *Sport, Economy and Society in Britain 1750–1914* Cambridge: Cambridge University Press, 1998

Tremlett, George *Clubmen: the history of the Working Men's Club and Institute Union* London: Secker and Warburg, 1987

Wade, Eileen K. *Olave Baden-Powell* London: Hodder and Stoughton, 1971

Ward, Irene *FANY Invicta* London: Hutchinson, 1953

Weinreb, Ben and Hibbert, Christopher *The London Encyclopaedia* London: Macmillan, 1983

Williams, Cicely *Women on the Rope* London: Allen and Unwin, 1973

Williams, Jean *A Game for Rough Girls? A history of women's football in Britain* London: Routledge, 2003

Willis, Evelyn 'Ladies' Clubs in London' in: *Lady's Realm* (January 1899)

Women in Sport ed. Gerda L. Cohen Newbury Park, CA: Sage, 1993

Women of the RAFOCA, no. 236 (January–April 1942)

Wood, Christopher 'Brooks's since the Second World War' in: Ziegler, P. and Seward, D. (eds) *Brooks's* London: Constable, 1991

Woodbridge, George *The Reform Club, 1836–1978* London: Reform Club, 1978

WRAF Old Comrades' Association News Letter, v. 22 (December 1939)

The Wren: the magazine of the Association of Wrens – Triennial: 1921–

Ziegler, Philip and Seward, Desmond (eds) *Brooks's* London: Constable, 1991

Index

Lightning Source UK Ltd.
Milton Keynes UK
23 January 2010

149020UK00002B/14/P